Tablets
of
Stone

JOHN G. REISINGER

Cover design by Arthur L. Furtado

Crowne Publications, Inc.
P.O. Box 688
Southbridge, Massachusetts 01550

Printed in the United States of America

ISBN 0-925703-05-2

Acknowledgements

To an Army General, a social security administrator, a waste management specialist, a postal carrier, several engineers, a contractor, a court clerk, who continually encouraged me and prayed for the ministry of *Sound of Grace* and to my wife who wonders what life would be like without a computer and word processor occupying most of her husband's time.

Author's Preface

In this book we are going to study the place and function of the Ten Commandments in redemptive history as this plan unfolds in the OT Scriptures, moves into the NT Scriptures, and finally reaches into the life of the Church today. The material will be of special interest to those concerned with the relationship between law and grace. Hopefully, we will be able to give some clear Biblical answers that will help the average Christian to obey the command "Be ye holy, for I am holy." If this book helps any of God's people to better understand His Word and thereby be led to love and serve our Lord Jesus Christ more fervently, we will be well rewarded for our efforts.

Table of Contents

CHAPTER 1

The Necessity Of Using Biblical Terminology

Before we can state what the Bible *means*, we must first understand what it says. In this present study it is essential that we understand what the Word of God itself says about the Ten Commandments. We should always begin the study of any Biblical doctrine with a clear understanding of the terminology used by the Holy Spirit. Thus we will first look up the meaning of the words "Ten Commandments" in all the texts of Scripture where those words are used. We will then look at the synonyms that are used for the Ten Commandments. This will give us a clear Biblical picture of the words which God wrote on stone tables at Mt. Sinai.

Where do the words the "Ten Commandments" first appear in the Bible?

The first occurrences of these words are in Exodus 34:28 when the Ten Commandments were written on the tablets of stone and given to the nation of Israel. Here is the verse and context:

> *And the LORD said unto Moses, Write thou **these words:** for after the **tenor of these words** I have made a **covenant** with thee and with Israel. And he was there with the LORD forty days and forty nights; he did*

1

*neither eat bread, nor drink water. And he wrote upon
the tables the **words of the** covenant, the ten commandments.*[1]

Ex. 34:27,28

The significance of the words "Ten Commandments"
occurring for the first time in Scripture at Sinai will be made
clear as we proceed with this study. For now, we can say that
the first time in Scripture we are introduced to the words "Ten
Commandments," we are told the following things:

1. The Ten Commandments were written on Tablets
   of Stone by God Himself.
2. This event occurred at Mt Sinai when God entered
   a special and unique covenant relationship with the
   nation of Israel.
3. The Ten Commandments were the specific terms,
   or "words of the covenant" that were written on
   the Tables of Stone at Mt. Sinai: "He wrote upon
   the tables the *words of the covenant, the ten commandments.*"
4. The Ten Commandments, or covenant, was made
   only with the nation of Israel: "I have made a
   covenant with thee and with **Israel.**"

These four things are always associated with the words "Ten
Commandments" when those words, or their synonyms, are
used in the Bible. The Ten Commandments equals the "words
of the covenant," and this covenant is always associated with
the Tables of Stone given to Israel at Sinai. This is the uniform and consistent teaching of the Word of God. Neither the
Old Testament Scriptures nor the New Testament Scriptures
will ever change what is said about the Ten Commandments
in this text. The nature and function of the Ten Command-

---

[1]The use of bold letters within a quotation means that I am emphasizing something that
the writer being quoted did not emphasize.

ments will always be consistent with the first mention of them in the Bible.

It is essential that we remember these Biblical four facts as set forth in the verse that first introduces us to the words "Ten Commandments." We should tatoo on our brain that "Israel," "Ten Commandments," "Mt Sinai," "Tablets of Stone" and "words of the covenant," are phrases that always go together in the Word of God. Any discussion of the Ten Commandments that in any way separates them from the "words of the covenant" written on the Tables of Stone and given to Israel at Sinai is not following Scripture. All we need to do is to read this verse and to listen to what is being said and we will be well on our way to understanding the nature and function of the Ten Commandments in the history of redemption.

How common is the use of the words "Ten Commandments" in the Bible?

The words "Ten Commandments" are used only three times in the whole Bible. They are used in Ex. 34:28 quoted above), Dt. 4:13 and Dt. 10:4:

*And he declared unto you his covenant, which he com-manded you to perform, even the **ten commandments**; and he wrote them upon two **tables of stone.***

Dt. 4:13

*And he **wrote on the tables**, according to the first writ-ing, the **ten commandments**, which the **LORD** spake unto you in the mount out of the midst of the fire in the day of the assembly. . . .*

Dt. 10:4

These texts repeat the same facts given in Ex. 34:28. Dt. 4:13 is even more emphatic than Ex. 34 concerning the nature of the Ten Commandments. The verse starts with God "declaring his *covenant*" and then specifically emphasizes, by

using the word *"even,"* that the covenant made with Israel was
the *Ten Commandments.*

The NT Scriptures never once use the words "Ten Commandments," nor do any of the OT prophets use these words
in any of their teaching, rebukes, or exhortations. The writers
of the Psalms have much to say about "law" and
"commandments" but none of them, including the author of
Psalm 119, ever use the words "the Ten Commandments."

As can be seen, the only references in the whole Bible to
the "Ten Commandments" *as a unit,* or a specific document,
are the three verses connected with Israel at Mt. Sinai when
the Ten Commandments were written with the finger of God
on the Tablets of Stone and given to Israel as the terms of
a covenant. It is essential that the words "The Ten Commandments" always be thought of as a single unit or document. The
individual commandments continue in force, as individual and
specific commandments, long after the Tables of Stone end
as a covenant. We will say more about this fact later.

> **Are there other terms used in the Bible that are
> synonymous and interchangeable with the words
> "Ten Commandments?"**

There are at least seven other words or phrases that are
used to refer to the Ten Commandments, or "words of the
covenant". We will list them one at a time and give a sample
of the references. The first reference for each phrase will usually be the first reference in Scripture where the phrase is
found. The same will be true of the last reference for each
phrase. It will greatly help us to understand the nature and
function of the Ten Commandments if we realize that we can
substitute any of the following terms in place of the words "Ten
Commandments." All seven phrases mean exactly the same
thing when used in the Bible.

1. **The Tables of Stone:** This is the most common way that
   the Bible refers to the Ten Commandments. This usually
   surprises people who have never carefully looked at how

the Holy Spirit refers to the words written with God's finger at Sinai. Let us look at some specific texts of Scripture:

*And the LORD said unto Moses, Come up to me into the mount, and be there: and I will give thee **tables of stone**, and a law, and commandments which I have written; that thou mayest teach them.*

Ex. 24:12

*And he declared unto you **his covenant**, which he commanded you **to perform**, even **ten commandments**; and he wrote them upon two **tables of stone.***

Dt. 4:13

And the LORD delivered unto me two tables of stone written with the finger of God; and on them was written according to all the words, which the LORD spake with you in the mount out of the midst of the fire in the day of the assembly.

Dt. 9:10

*There was nothing in the ark save the two **tables of stone,** which Moses put there at Horeb, **when** the LORD made a **covenant** with the children of Israel, **when** they came out of the land of Egypt.*

I Kings 8:9

*Forasmuch as ye are manifestly declared to be the epistle of Christ ministered by us, written not with ink, but with the Spirit of the living God; not in **tables of stone**, but in fleshy tables of the heart.*

II Cor. 3:3

Again, we note that every reference in the Bible to "the Tables of Stone," like the synonymous words "the Ten Commandments," is connected to Mt. Sinai when the commandments were written on the Tables of Stone and given to Israel as a covenant. This is the uniform meaning that the Holy Spirit gives to the Ten Commandments when they are spoken of as a unit regardless of which particular term is used. The "Ten Commandments" and the "Tables of Stone" are one and the same thing. From now on in this book we will follow the practice of the writers of Scripture and freely interchange the words "Tables of Stone," or any of the other synonyms, when referring to the words "Ten Commandments."

2. **The Tables of Testimony:** This term is only used twice and is found both times in the Book of Exodus. Again, both references refer to Sinai when the "Tables of Testimony" (Ten Commandments) were given as a written record of the covenant conditions that would be used as the legal "testimony" against Israel if they broke the covenant. We do not ever remember this Biblical term being applied to the Ten Commandments by any preacher or writer. Such an omission is most unfortunate. Here are the two textual references:

*And he gave unto Moses, when he had made an end of communing with him upon mount Sinai, two **tables of testimony**, tables of stone, written with the finger of God.*

Ex. 31:18

*When Moses came down from mount Sinai with the two **tablets of Testimony** in his hand, he was not aware that his face was radiant because he had spoken with the Lord.*

Ex. 34:29

The term "Tables of Testimony," like the preceding two terms, is always connected with God's dealing with the nation of Israel at Mt Sinai when He entered into the special covenant relationship with them. The "Ten Commandments," the "Tables of Stone," and the "Tables of Testimony" are one and the same thing in the Scriptures.

3. **The Testimony:** The word "Testimony" is used in two verses to describe the Ten Commandments. The first in-

stance is when God gave Moses instructions concerning building the Ark of the Covenant to house the "Testimony," or the Ten Commandments. The other time is when the Ark was finished and the Ten Commandments were put into the Ark. Here are the texts:

*The spokes are to remain in the rings of this ark; they are not to be removed. Then put in the ark the **Testimony**, which I will give you.*

Ex. 25:15,16.

*He took the **Testimony** and placed it in the ark. . . .*

Ex. 40:20

It is significant that the word "Testimony" is singular even though there were "Ten" commandments written on the tablets. It confirms that the Ten Commandments are considered to be one single document, and the document is the covenant, or "Testimony," between God and Israel. We could read the above verses and substitute either the word "Covenant" or the words "Ten Commandments" for "Testimony" since they all mean exactly the same thing.

4. **The First Covenant:** The fourth term which is used as a synonym of the "Ten Commandments" is the words "First Covenant." This phrase is used in the Bible only twice but it is implied in other places where the New Covenant is contrasted to the Old, or first, Covenant that it replaced. The covenant described in the words "the covenant I made with their fathers" in passages like Jer. 31:33 and Heb. 8 through 10 is clearly the "first" covenant, or Ten Commandments, that was given at Sinai on the tables of stone. Here are the texts:

*For if that **first covenant** had been faultless, then should no place have been sought for the **second [covenant]**.*

Heb. 8:7

*Then verily the **first covenant** had also ordinances of divine service, and a worldly sanctuary.*[2]

Heb. 9:1

Again, as in all of the other instances, the references connect the "First Covenant" with the giving of the Ten Commandments on the Tables of Stone to the nation of Israel at Mt. Sinai as a covenant. The "Ten Commandments," the "Tables of Stone," the "Tables of Testimony" and the "First Covenant" are one and the same in the Scriptures.

5. **The Old Covenant:** The fifth term used to refer to the Ten Commandments written on stone is "the Old Covenant." The term is clearly implied in Heb 8:6 where three distinct contrasts are made. There is a contrast between the following things:

1. the *ministries* of Aaron and Christ;

2. the two *covenants* upon which the two ministries are based; and

3. the superiority of the *"better promises"* upon which the New Covenant is established. The Old Covenant said "do and live/disobey and die" but the New says "it is finished/believe."

Notice how these three comparisons are set forth in the argument developed by the writer of Hebrews:

*But the [1] **ministry** Jesus has received is as superior to theirs as [2] **the covenant of which he is mediator** is to the old [covenant] one, and it is founded on*

---

[2]It is essential that we do not confuse the actual covenant (the Tablets of Stone) with all of the laws and ceremonies that administered the covenant. It is clear from both the OT Scriptures and Heb 9:1-5, that the "First Covenant" was the Tables of the Covenant, or the Ten Commandments, and everything else was part of the services and rituals that administered the covenant.

*[3] **better promises.** For if there had been nothing wrong with that **first covenant,** no place would been sought for **another [covenant].***

Heb 8:6,7 NIV

It is the obvious result of these comparisons that demonstrates why the Old Covenant written on the Tablets of Stone had to be replaced by the "new and better" covenant. The same truth is found in Heb 8:13:

*In that he saith, a **new covenant,** he hath made the **first [covenant] old.** Now that which decayeth and waxeth old is ready to vanish away.*

Heb 8:13 NIV

The NIV correctly translates the Greek with "covenant" in II Cor 3:14 instead of "testament" as in the KJV:

*But their minds were made dull, for to this day the same veil remains when the **old covenant** is read. It has not been removed, because only in Christ is it taken away.*

II Cor 3:14

As in all of the previous instances, the term "Old Covenant" is always a reference to the Ten Commandments written on the Tablets of Stone and given to Israel at Sinai as a covenant. If II Cor 3:14 is referring to the Old Testament *Scriptures*, it is the exception. However, the context is comparing two different ministries based on two different kinds of covenants. It is not comparing two different kinds of Scriptures. The "Ten Commandments," the "Tables of Stone," the "Tables of Testimony," the "First Covenant," and the "Old Covenant" are one and the same thing in the Scriptures.

Some theologians do not understand that the "Old Covenant" refers to the covenant that God made with Israel at Mt. Sinai. They thus deny that Christ replaced the Old Covenant with a "new and better" covenant. They insist on trying to push the Old Covenant back into the garden of Eden.

Professor John Murray, one of the greatest theologians in this century, is the rare exception. He not only says that the Old Covenant is the Sinaitic, Professor Murray also chides those who try to connect it with a supposed "covenant of works" with Adam. His statement of the case is clear:

> This administration [Adamic] has often been denoted **the Covenant of Works. . . .** It is not designated a covenant in Scripture. Hosea 6:7 **may be interpreted otherwise** and does not provide the basis for such a construction of the Adamic economy. . . . It should never be confused with what the Scripture calls the old covenant or first covenant (cf. Jer. 31:31-34; 2 Cor. 3:14; Heb.8:7,13). The first or old covenant **is the Sinaitic.** And not only must this confusion in denotation be avoided, but also any attempt to **interpret the Mosaic covenant in terms of the Adamic institution.** The latter could only apply to the state of innocency, and to Adam alone as a representative head. The view that in the Mosaic covenant there is a repetition of the so-called covenant of works, current among covenant theologians, is a grave misconception and involves an **erroneous conception** of the Mosaic covenant. . . . [3]

6. **The Words of the Covenant:** The sixth synonym used by the Holy Spirit for "the Ten Commandments" is the phrase "the words of the Covenant." These words establish beyond question that the Ten Commandments are the covenant document that established Israel as a nation, or body politic, at Mt. Sinai. The Ten Commandments are expressly called "the words of the **covenant.**" Notice this fact in the following text:

And he was there with the LORD forty days and forty

---

[3]Collected Writings of John Murray, Vol. 4, pg 49,50, Banner of Truth.

*nights; he did neither eat bread, nor drink water. And he wrote upon the tables the **words of the covenant, the ten commandments.***

Ex 34:28

Again, as in the previous five cases, the text references the "words of the covenant" back to Mt Sinai when God gave the Ten Commandments to Israel as a covenant. This fact is inescapable in these texts. They explicitly state that the *"words of the covenant"* were the *Ten Commandments.* The Ten Commandments, the "Tables of Stone," the "Tables of Testimony," the "First Covenant," the "Old Covenant" and the "words of the covenant" are all one and the same in the Scriptures. They are all interchangeable terms.

7. **The Tables of the Covenant.** The seventh phrase that the Bible uses as a synonym for the Ten Commandments is the "Tables of the Covenant." Moses used this phrase at the second giving of the law in Deut. It is very obvious that Moses wanted to impress the word "Covenant" on Israel's mind when he reminds them of God giving the Ten Commandments as the terms of the covenant written on the Tables of the Covenant. It is not possible to read the following instructions of Moses without seeing that the Tables of the Covenant are the exact same thing as the Ten Commandments:

*When I was gone up into the mount to receive the tables of stone, even the **tables of the covenant** which the LORD made with you, then I abode in the mount forty days and forty nights, I neither did eat bread nor drink water: And the LORD delivered unto me **two tables of stone** written with the finger of God; and on them was written according to all the words, which the LORD spake with you in the mount out of the midst of the fire in the day of the assembly. And it came to pass at the end of forty days and forty nights, that the LORD gave me the **two tables of stone**, even the*

tables of the covenant.

Deut. 9:9-11

The subject of the message given by Moses on this occasion concerns God, at Sinai, giving the Tablets of the covenant upon which was written the Ten Commandments.

The NIV, in one instance adds the word "stone" to this phrase and the Ten Commandments are called the "stone tables of the covenant." This occurs in Hebrews:

> . . . *which had the golden altar of incense and the gold-covered ark of the covenant. This ark contained the gold jar of manna, Aaron's staff that had budded, and the* **stone tablets of the covenant.**

Heb. 9:4

The ninth chapter of the Book of Hebrews contrasts the ministry of Aaron in the earthly Tabernacle in the midst of Israel with the ministry of Christ in the true Tabernacle in Heaven itself. The word "covenant" is again the recurring theme in this chapter. Verse 4 tells us that the stone Tables of the Covenant were kept in the Ark of the Covenant in the Most Holy Place behind the veil. We remember that not only the Ark but the *whole Tabernacle* was designed in reference to the Tables of the Covenant. All of the sacrifices and all of the ministry of the priests centered around the Ten Commandment in the Ark. The whole system illustrated the truth that they was no approach to God until the terms of the Covenant in Ark had been met:

> *The Holy Spirit was showing by this that the way into the Most Holy Place had* **not yet been disclosed** *as long as the first tabernacle was still standing. This is an illustration for the present time, indicating that the gifts and sacrifices being offered were* **not able to clear the conscience** *of the worshiper.*

Heb. 9:8,9

The inability of all of the ministries connected with the Old

Covenant to "cleanse the *conscience*" is always, as in this verse, connected with "the way into the Most Holy Place" being closed off.

The writer of Hebrews shows that the "once for all" sacrifice of Christ overcame this inability and forever opened up the way into the Most Holy Place. This truth is shown by contrasting the greater effect of the better sacrifice of Christ with the ineffectual sacrifice of animals. The key verse is 15. It tells us the specific reason for the need of the New Covenant to be established in nothing less than the shed blood of the Son of God Himself:

> *For this reason [to effect what the Old Covenant could not] Christ is the mediator of a **new covenant,** that those who are called may receive the promised eternal [not just one year] inheritance—**now** that he has died [under the curse of the covenant in the Ark] as a ransom to set them free [Gal 4:4-6) from the sins **committed under the first covenant.***

Heb. 9:15

None of the sins against the Old Covenant were truly atoned for until the actual death of Christ on Calvary it is the atoning work of Christ that gave Him the right to send the gift of the Holy Spirit. The coming of the Holy Spirit on the day of Pentecost was the heart of the promise in the Old Testament Scriptures. However, that promise could not be fulfilled as long as the Tabernacle was still standing, and the Tabernacle must stand as long as the Old Covenant (Ten Commandments) in the Ark of the Covenant were in force as the covenant foundation of God's relationship to Israel. It all stands or falls together.

As in the other six examples, we see again that the same ingredients always go together when the Ten Commandments or one of their synonyms are used. The "Ten Commandments," the "Tables of Stone," "the Tables of the Testimony", the "Testimony," The "First Covenant," the "Old Covenant," the

"words of the covenant" and the "stone Tables of the Covenant" all mean exactly the same thing in the Bible. All eight
of these terms are interchangeable. We doubt that anyone can
look at the preceding verses and question what has been said.
As we will see later, some people may have difficulty with ap-
plying this truth to theology. For instance, if a person says,
"I believe the Ten Commandments are the rule of life for a
Christian today," that person should realize that he is also say-
ing, "I believe the stone Tablets of the Covenant kept in the
Ark of the Covenant are the Christian's rule of life for today."
Both statement mean *exactly* the same thing according to the
Bible.

The first time we listed on a chalk board the preceding
seven terms that are synonymous with the words "the Ten Commandments," a man asked, "Why did you not list some of the
verses in the Bible that speak of 'the moral law' when referring to the Ten Commandments?" He was quite surprised when
we replied, "No such references were listed simply because *there
are none*"! The Bible does not even *use* the term "moral law"
let alone *equate such a term with the Ten Commandments*.

We may be jumping ahead a bit, but it might be well to
mention the fact that the term "moral law" is a theological
term developed in the Middle Ages and is not a Biblical term
in any sense whatsoever. The term may, or may not, be a correct and useful term if it can be proven to be Scripturally correct. However, the term would first have to be established with
texts of Scripture that clearly prove the doctrine implied or
stated in the term. We have never seen this attempted with
the term "moral law." We will discuss the term later. At this
point we are only interested in what the Word of God itself
says and not in non-Biblical terms developed by theologians
as the essential means necessary to teach their particular system of theology. Our question is this: How does God Himself
want us to think and speak about the words "the Ten Commandments?" The answer is simple if we follow the Holy Spirit's
example in the Bible and use the terminology that He has in-

spired. We will always think "covenant."

Perhaps it would be good to take all the above texts of Scripture that use the seven different terms as synonyms when referring to the Ten Commandments and summarize exactly what the Bible itself says about the Ten Commandments. The following statement is nothing but Bible texts put together into one definitive statement of the way the Bible treats the Tablets of Stone:

> God entered into a special and unique covenant relationship with the nation of Israel at Mt Sinai. The terms of that covenant are sometimes called the **Ten Commandments.** The Ten Commandments are also called The **First Covenant**, especially when that covenant is contrasted with the **New Covenant** that replaces it. The First, or **Old Covenant** was made only with the nation of Israel at Mt. Sinai. The actual **"words of the Covenant"** are the **Ten Commandments** as they are written on **Tables of Stone** with the finger of God. This covenant document is also called the **Old Covenant.** It is also called the **Tables of Testimony,** or just the **Testimony.** The terms **"Ten Commandments,"** "Tables of Stone," "Tables of **Testimony,"** **"Testimony," "Old Covenant," "First Covenant,"** "words of the covenant,"and "stone **Tables of the Covenant"** are one and the same in the Scriptures. All eight terms mean exactly the same thing and they are all interchangeable with each other.

If this statement causes either confusion in our thinking or problems with our theology, we are not thinking in Biblical terms when we think of the Ten Commandments. If the clear Biblical facts set forth in the verses of Scripture we have previously quoted, and just now summarized *in the words of Scripture* in the above statement, are totally new to us, then our thinking in reference to the Ten Commandments is not Biblical! We repeat, we must learn to use *Biblical terminology.*

We should start our study of any Bible doctrine with a clear understanding of the actual verses of Scriptures that discuss that specific subject. I have yet to see a discussion of the Ten Commandments that lists and discusses the Biblical references to the Ten Commandments as we have just done.

Most people are amazed that the NT Scriptures never once use the words "Ten Commandments." It is obvious that these people, when they study the subject of the "Ten Commandments," never bother to look up the actual verses in the Bible where God Himself speaks about "the Ten Commandments." Perhaps if they would have done this just once then some of their conclusions, and surely their terminology, would be radically different.

Summary

The Bible always relates the Ten Commandments to Israel at Mt Sinai. The Ten Commandments were the "words of the covenant" that were written on the Tables of Stone and put in the Ark of the Covenant. The terms "Ten Commandments," "Tables of Stone," "Tables of Testimony," "First Covenant," "Old Covenant," "Tables of the Covenant," and "words of the covenant" are all one and the same thing in the Scriptures. They are all interchangeable terms.

We are never told or encouraged to think of "unchanging moral law" when we read the words "Ten Commandments" or any of the synonymous terms. We are to think "covenant." We are to think of a specific code of law (the Ten Commandments) that was made the specific terms of a covenant document. We are to always remember that the Ten Commandments were the specific terms, written on stone tablets, of the covenant that established Israel's special relationship with God. The Ten Commandments, Israel, Sinai, Covenant all go together. They all began at the same time and they all ended at the same time.

The individual duties commanded in the various commandments are a different story. The Ten Commandments, considered as a covenant document, have been replaced by the New Covenant. The individual commandments stand, fall, or are changed according to their own nature and merit. Nine of them are clearly repeated, with some changes, in the New Testament Scriptures and therefore just as binding today as when given at Sinai.

CHAPTER 2

Problem of "Two Versions"

The second thing by way of introduction concerns the necessity of being sure that we know exactly what was written on the Tables of Stone. It is impossible to understand the theological significance of the Tables of the Covenant if we do not know exactly what is being commanded in the terms of the covenant. We must first know exactly what duty is being commanded before we start discussing its nature and purpose. Nothing but confusion and misunderstanding can result if we are not all talking about the same thing.

What was written on the Tablets of Stone?
Exactly what are the "Ten Commandments?"

What was the exact content of the Old Covenant that was written with the finger of God on the Tables of the Covenant? One would think that such a question need not be asked and some may be surprised that we start with something so "simple." The very fact that no one starts here and just "assumes" that everyone knows the answer is indicative of the amount of ignorance there is about the Ten Commandments and the bad theologies that has been produced by that ignorance.

First of all, it must be noted that the Bible gives two *different "versions"* of the Ten Commandments that were written on the Tables of Stone. And there are some very real differences in the two accounts. The following chart compares some of the differences in the two versions of the Ten Commandments as they are found in Exodus twenty and Deuteronomy five. The first through third and the sixth through ninth commandments are almost identical. The greatest differences are in the fourth and fifth. Since our concern at this point is only in the fact that there *are* two different versions of the Ten Commandments, we will only note the differences in the fourth commandment.

A dotted line (.......) means that something is missing in that particular account, and words in *italics* means that something has been added that is not in the other account. We need only to glance at the amount of dotted lines and words in italics to see that there is a vast difference in the two different accounts of the fourth commandment. We find it hard to believe that these differences are almost totally ignored by theologians:

EXODUS 20	DEUTERONOMY 5
8. Remember the sabbath day, to keep it holy.	12. Keep the sabaath day to sanctify it, as the Lord thy God hath commanded thee.
. . . .	
9. Six days shalt thou labor, and do all thy work;	13. Six days thou shalt labor, and do all thy work:
10. But the seventh day is the sabbath of the Lord thy God: in it thou shalt not do any work, thou, nor thy son, nor thy daughter, thy manservant, nor thy maidservant,	14. But the seventh day is the sabbath of the LORD thy God in it thou shalt not do any work, thou, nor thy son, thy daughter, not thy manservant, nor thy maidservant,
. . . .	*nor thine ox, not thine ass,*

nor thy cattle, nor thy stranger that is within thy gates:

....

....
....
....

nor any of thy cattle, nor thy stranger that is within thy gates;

that thy manservant and thy maidservant may rest as well as thou.

11. For in six days the Lord made heaven and earth, the sea, and all that in them is, and rested the seventh day: wherefore the Lord blessed the sabbath day, and hallowed it.

....
....
....
....
....
....
....

....
....
....
....
....
....
....
....
....

15. And remember that thou wast a servant in the land of Egypt, and that the LORD thy God brought thee out thence through a mighty hand and by a stretched out arm: therefore the LORD thy God commanded thee to keep the sabbath day.

It is very obvious there is a great difference in the fourth commandment as recorded in Ex. 20:8-11 and the same commandment as recorded in Dt. 5:12-15. Moses clearly gave two totally different reasons for why the Sabbath was to be kept holy. The first reason was to follow God's example in Genesis and the second was to remember the recent deliverance from Egypt. Very few writers even mention these differences in the two versions of the Ten Commandments, and most of them make no attempt to deal with the obvious problems created by the impossibility of having *two different things* written on the same *Tables of Stone*.

A.W. Pink, in his commentary on Exodus, never notices

the problem. Walter Chantry, in *God's Righteous Kingdom*, not only does not mention the fact there are differences, he also uses Deut. 5:22 in a manner that greatly compounds the problem.[4] Chantry insists that when Moses said, "and He added nothing more" that God explicitly meant that "nothing can be added" to the commandments recorded in Deut 5:1-21. This means that none of the things found in Ex. 20 that are omitted in Dt. 5 can be *added* to Dt. 5 and then considered to be part of the actual commandment written on stone. Patrick Fairbairn, in *The Revelation of God in Scripture,* is the only writer that makes any kind of a serious attempt to resolve the problem.[5] Fairbairn does not mention the further problem created by Deut. 5:22.

We think it is more than fair to say that any attempt to understand the true meaning and function of the Tablets of Stone in the history of redemption that does not begin by clearly establishing exactly what was written on those tablets is doomed to confusion and contradiction. How is it possible to know the true meaning and significance of commandments when we do not know for sure what a given commandment actually says? Likewise, we feel justified in thinking that a person's understanding of the significance of the Ten Commandments is rather shallow if that person never even noticed that the Bible gives two different versions of those commandments.

What Is Involved in the Fact that there are "Two Different Versions" of the Ten Commandments in the Bible?

One: The Verbal Inspiration of the Scripture. We are not talking about two versions of a parable or miracle. We are dealing with very special and unique commandments of great sig-

---

[4]See pages 87,88 of God's Righteous Kingdom, by Walter Chantry, Banner of Truth.
[5]See page 325 in The Revelation of God in Scripture, Patrick Fairbairn, Guardian Press.

nificance that were written in stone by the finger of God. Nothing could be more exact and specific than that. It is not possible that God wrote on the Tablets of Stone everything found in *both* the Exodus 20 version and the Deut. 5 version of the Ten Commandments. Something is obviously wrong and an awful lot is at stake until the problem is solved. The solution might be a bit easier if two different writers had given the two different versions. However, in this case Moses is the author of both Ex. 20 and Dt. 5.

Patrick Fairbairn uses the basic "dynamic equivalent" theory to reconcile the two versions. This means that a writer may use a different word or phrase in two different accounts of the same thing but the basic meaning of the two are the same. Even if this method is accepted as legitimate, it could not be stretched to reconcile the radical differences in Ex. 20 and Deut. 5. How can God delivering Israel from Egypt in any way be the "dynamic equivalent" of God creating the heavens and earth in six days and then resting on the seventh day?

Believing that the Ten Commandments, *as given in Exodus 20 and* Dt. 5, are the "eternal unchanging moral law of God" only adds to the problem. Can anyone believe that God intended the Tablets of Stone to be what some preachers insist, with no Biblical proof, on calling "the unchanging moral law," and also believe that God would inspire Moses to give *two different versions* of His "unchanging moral law?" This fact alone ought to alert any serious mind to stop and think. One thing is certain, the two different versions of the Ten Commandments must be reconciled to each other before it is possible to know for sure what was actually written on the Tablets of Stone! We have people arguing vehemently about "unchanging laws" without even knowing what those laws actually say.

There are basically only three possible approaches to the problem of the two different versions of the Ten Commandments:

1. The Bible contradicts itself. Every Christian will reject this explanation.

2. Moses, in Deut. 5, "forgot" what God actually wrote
    on the Tablets of Stone in Ex. 20 and therefore
    left out the part about creation (Fairbairn is really
    weak on this point). Moses also "added," in Deut.
    5, the part about deliverance from Egypt even
    though it was not actually part of the original Ten
    Commandments given in Ex. 20. It is obvious we
    must also reject this explanation. It is a "rational"
    version of the first approach.
3. All that was actually written on the Tablets of Stone
    was the bare commandments. In the case of the
    fourth commandment, all that was written on the
    tables was the words *"Remember the Sabbath Day
    to keep it holy."* All of the rest of the words re-
    lating to the actual observance of the Sabbath, in
    both Ex. 20 and Deut. 5, are commentary added
    by Moses and not part of the commandment itself
    as written on the Tablets of Stone.

The last solution is obviously the only position consistent
with verbal inspiration even though it might create some problems for some theologians. It would be most appropriate for
Moses, standing at Mt Sinai, to point Israel back to the God
of Creation as a ground for obeying the newly given covenant
sign, or Sabbath commandment. As we shall see, the seventh
day Sabbath was the specific "sign" of the Mosaic covenant
that established the nation of Israel as a body politic at Mt.
Sinai. It would also be just as appropriate for Moses to remind Israel (at the second giving of the law in Dt. 5) of God's
redemptive rights over Israel because of the recent deliverance by blood and power from Egypt. The two reasons together combine the creatorial rights and redemptive claims
of God over His chosen nation and furnish a double obligation for obeying the covenant sign and the whole covenant.
However, it is obvious that neither of the two different reasons
given by Moses for keeping the seventh day holy were part
of the actual commandments, or covenant, that was written

on the Tablets of Stone. Both reasons are commentary added by Moses to enforce the great significance of the covenant sign (Sabbath) that had just been given to Israel.

Two: As it regards the Sabbath Commandment. It is impossible to use Ex. 20:11 to prove that the seventh day Sabbath was a so-called "Creation Ordinance." You must "add" that to the version given in Deut. 5 before you can make it part of the actual commandment. However, as Walter Chantry has clearly demonstrated, Deut. 5:22 forbids any such additions.

1. God spake "these words" (Deut. 5:22) refers to the words just spoken in Deut. 5:1-21.
2. There is no mention at all of Creation in Deut. 5 just as there is no mention of deliverance from Egypt in Ex. 20
3. Moses is emphatic that God "added no more" to the words just written in Deut. 5:1-21.

The purpose of Chantry in the section where he quotes Deut. 5:22 is to prove the seventh day Sabbath is a Creation Ordinance. It is surprising that he did not realize that his comments on Dt. 5:22 were making it impossible to use Ex. 20:11 as proof that the Sabbath began at creation. In order for Ex. 20:11 to be part of the Fourth Commandment, Chantry must clearly show how he can add the words found in this verse to the account in Deut. 5 without admitting that the words "added no more" in Dt. 5:22 really do not mean "added no more." If anyone chooses to believe that the Sabbath commandment existed before Sinai, he must get his evidence from a source other than Ex. 20 and Dt. 5.

Three: Our Theological view of "Moral Law." As mentioned earlier, we must ask this question: "If God intended the Tables of Stone to be a revelation of His 'one unchanging moral law,' would He have given us *two different versions* of what He had written?" We think this is self contradictory. We need a whole new mind set that thinks and speaks in *Biblical terms* instead of *theological terms.* We need to say, "Give me a clear text of Scripture" instead of accepting theological terms as equal to Scripture verses. We must quit referring to the Ten Commandments as the "unchanging moral law of God" and begin to think and speak of them the same way the Bible does. We must call them, as the writers of Scripture do, the "Tables of the Covenant" or one of the other synonyms. When ever we hear the words "the Ten Commandments" our first thought should automatically be "the words of the Old Covenant written on the Tables of Stone at Mt Sinai." Until we do this, we are failing to think and speak in Biblical terms.

We are not suggesting that there are no "moral laws" written on the Tablets of Stone. The Ten Commandments *contain much*, actually *mostly*, moral law that is just as binding on a Christian today as it was on Moses. However, that is totally different than saying "the Ten Commandments, as written on the Tablets of Stone, are **"THE** eternal unchanging moral law."

We simply must fix in our minds that the Bible always treats the "Ten Commandments" as a single unit, or codified list that constitutes a covenant document. And that document is the Decalogue, or "Ten Words." When that covenant ended, everything it represented was also ended. However, the specific moral duties commanded in the individual commandments written on those tables are another thing altogether. Nine of the ten individual commandments are clearly repeated by both our Lord in the Gospels and by the Apostles in the Epistles.

Everything that God commands is "moral law" to the individual commanded. To pick up sticks on the Sabbath was one of the most immoral things that a man could do under the Old Covenant. This was not because there is anything inherently wrong with picking up sticks. The man was stoned to death because the Fourth Commandment, which was the covenant sign, specifically forbid any physical labor on the seventh day. A commandment that was ceremonial in nature became the highest moral duty possible when God made it the sign of the covenant. We will say more about this in a later chapter.

It was not immoral for a man to take a second wife under the same Old Covenant that had the man stoned to death for gathering sticks. The same "Book of The Covenant" that commanded "keep the Sabbath holy" also *commanded* a man to sleep with *both wives* when he took the *second wife* (Ex. 21:10).

The exact opposite is true of the above two examples under the New Covenant. The ceremonial sign, or Sabbath, of the Old Covenant ceased when the covenant, of which it was a sign, was done away in Christ. The Seventh Commandment was changed by Christ, the new Lawgiver, and polygamy is now considered adultery. Polygamy was not a sin against the so called "moral law of God" according to the covenant under which David lived, but it is a sin according to the New Covenant under which a Christian lives today. The Bible defines moral duty according to the laws of the specific covenant under which an individual lives and never by an imaginary code of "unchanging moral law."

Summary

The fact that there are *two different versions* of the Ten Commandments in the Bible presents some problems. There was a lot less written on the Tables of Stone than most people realize. The Ex. 20 version and the Dt. 5 version gives two different versions of the Sabbath Commandment. It seems improvable to us that God meant us to think of the Ten Commandments as His "unchanging moral law" when we are not positively sure what those commandments actually say. The covenant under which an individual lives defines that individual's duty to God. What was a "moral" duty to Israel is not necessarily a "moral" duty to a Christian. The Christian is given a much higher moral code under the new covenant simply because of greater demands and the power of grace.

CHAPTER 3

The Ten Commandments Are
A "Covenant"

T he Scriptures clearly and consistently call the Ten Commandments a "covenant" and treat them as a *distinct* and *separate* covenant. We have already seen this spelled out clearly in several texts of Scripture. However, despite the abundant textual evidence of this fact in the Scriptures, some theologians still cannot admit that the Ten Commandments form a separate and distinct covenant. Their basic presupposition that there is only "one covenant with two administrations" make it impossible for them to think or speak of the Ten Commandments as a distinct and separate covenant. To do so would destroy the very foundation of their system of theology. In that system, the "Mosaic arrangement" or "Mosaic administration"[6] could not possibly be a separate covenant, especially a *legal* covenant. The "Mosaic transaction" has to be an "administration of the one covenant of grace." However, the Word of God is quite clear that the Ten Commandments were the specific terms of a distinct and separate covenant. Here are several verses that clearly establish this point:

---

[6]These are the expressions used by theologians who fail to use Biblical terminology. Whenever a writer uses "arrangement," "administration" or "transaction" instead of "covenant to describe what happened at Sinai, he is not being exegetically correct.

*So He declared to you His **covenant** which He **commanded you to perform**, that is, the **Ten Commandments;** and He wrote them on two **tablets of stone.***
                                                                    Deut. 4:13

*When I went up in to the mountains to receive the **tablets of stone,** even the **tablets** of the **covenant** which the Lord had made with you . . . and the Lord gave me the two **tablets of stone** written with the finger of God . . . the Lord gave me the two **tablets of stone,** even the **tablets of the covenant.***
                                                                    Deut. 9:9-11

*Then the Lord said to Moses, "Write down these words, for **in accordance with these words** I have made a **covenant** with you and with Israel." Moses was there with the Lord forty days and forty nights without eating bread or drinking water. And he wrote on the **tablets the words of the covenant — the Ten Commandments.***
                                                                    Ex. 34:27,28.

How can anyone read the above verses and be honest with the words used and then deny that the Ten Commandments were the very "words" of a distinct and specific covenant? A system of theology built on non-biblical terms that refuses to use Biblical terms should be suspect. When a person uses terms that are both peculiar and essential to his particular system of theology we should be suspect of both the man and his system.

It is impossible to even begin to understand the nature and function of the Ten Commandments in redemptive history until we begin where God's Word itself begins. We must start by using the terminology that the Holy Spirit has been pleased to use. When we do this, we will automatically think and speak of the Ten Commandments as first and foremost being a distinct *covenant*. If our theological system forbids that, or even makes it unnatural or difficult, then it should be obvious that our system is not Biblical at that point.

The emphasis in the Word of God is always on the fact that the Tablets of Stone contain the terms of a covenant.

Remember that the Bible treats the "Ten Commandments," the "Tablets of the Covenant," the "Old Covenant" and the "words of the covenant" as equivalent and interchangeable terms. It is clear from all of the Biblical texts quoted in chapter one that God wants us to think "covenant" when there is a reference to either the words "Ten Commandments" or any of the seven synonymous terms used to describe them. It is simply impossible to think Biblically of the Ten Commandments apart from thinking of them as the "words of the covenant" written on the Tablets of Stone. Nowhere in the Bible are we instructed to think in terms of "**the unchanging moral law.**" Go back over the Biblical texts that refer to the Ten Commandments and see how clearly this truth is set forth in every single text. It is just as striking when the Tablets were smashed and the second set was made. It is not possible for the Bible to say any more clearly that the Ten Commandments are the exact words, or terms, of the Old Covenant than it does in the following verses:

> *When Moses approached the camp and saw the calf and the dancing, his anger burned and he threw the **tablets** out of his hands, breaking them in pieces. . . .*
> Ex. 32:18

> *The Lord said to Moses, "Chisel out two **stone tablets like the first ones,** and I will write on them the **words that were on the first tablets** which you broke. . . . "* *Then the Lord said, "**I am making a COVENANT with you. . . .** " Then the Lord said to Moses, "**Write down these words, for in accordance with them I have made a COVENANT with you** and with Israel. . . . And he wrote on the **tablets the words of***

the COVENANT — the TEN COMMANDMENTS.
Ex. 34:1,27,28

Summary

If our system of theology did not teach us to think about the Ten Commandments as a distinct and separate covenant then it did not teach us to think Scripturally. If we were taught to think of the Tablets of Stone as the "unchanging moral law of God," then we were taught wrong. Unfortunately, we were also taught, by default, to ignore the words and terms used by the Holy Spirit Himself. We may have done it unconsciously, but we nonetheless substituted erroneous theological terms in the place of Biblical terminology. Or even worse, if we were taught that the Ten Commandments simply *could not* be a separate distinct covenant but only a different *administration* of the so called Covenant of Grace, then we were taught to actually contradict the Word of God. The Holy Spirit *always* relates the Ten Commandments, when considered as a unit, with the "words of the covenant" that were written on the Tablets of Stone at Mt. Sinai.

CHAPTER 4

The Ten Commandments Are A "Legal" Covenant

T he Tablets of Stone, upon which were written the Ten Commandments, were not only a distinct covenant, they were the specific legal covenant that established Israel as a special nation before God at Mt Sinai. The Ark of the Covenant forever establishes the fact that the Ten Commandments were the specific document that constituted the legal covenant terms that was the basis of God's special relationship with the nation of Israel. The Ten Commandments were the actual "words of the covenant" that God made with Israel at Sinai. This fact is clearly stated in Ex. 34:27,28; Dt. 4:13, etc. The Ten Commandments were kept in the Ark of the Covenant only because they were the actual covenant document that established and maintained Israel's special status before God.

The very name of the box that housed the Ten Commandments and the special care given to that box clearly shows the true significance of the Tablets of Covenant, or Ten Commandments. No where does the Word of God even hint that the significance of the Ark of the Covenant was that it housed the so called "eternal unchanging moral law of God." It housed the **Old Covenant** that established Israel as a special nation before God and spelled out the terms (the Ten Commandments) of that relationship, or covenant. That box was not the

"Ark of the *Moral Law*." It was the "Ark of the *Covenant*," and the terms of the covenant was the Ten Commandments written on the Tablets of Stone and kept in the Ark. What can be more clear and simple?

The importance that Scripture attaches to the Ten Commandments is always, without a single exception, connected with Israel's special status before God as a unique nation.

Several verses of Scripture bring out this point clearly. One of the most important sections of Scripture in any discussion of the Ten Commandments is Exodus 19 through 24. Exodus 19 gives the preamble to the actual giving of the Ten Commandments in Ex. 20. Exodus 24 sets forth the official ratification of the "Book of the Covenant" with the sealing of blood. Many preachers and writers will emphasize the "grace" shown by God in delivering Israel from bondage in Egypt (Ex. 19:3,4) but totally ignore the next two verses (Ex. 19:5,6). While it is true that God showed special favor to the Jews in their redemption from Egypt, that was only a *physical redemption*. Most of those Israelites were still hard hearted sinners that needed to be convinced of their lost estate. God did **not** give the Ten Commandments to a "redeemed [regenerate] people for their sanctification." Such a view is not possible simply because those people were not *regenerate believers*. God gave the Ten Commandments as *a legal covenant of life and death* to a nation of proud sinners as a means of driving them to faith in the Gospel preached to Abraham.

As we shall see later, the function and goal of the Old Covenant (Ten Commandments) was a ministry of death by convicting the conscience of guilt.

We must not confuse the gracious *purpose* of God in giving the covenant at Sinai with the nature of the covenant itself. There was not an ounce of grace in the covenant itself but it was very gracious of God to give the covenant to Israel. It was the necessary instrument to bring conviction of sin and lead them to be saved by faith in the gospel preached to Abraham. The Tablets of Stone functioned in the conscience as a ministration of death by convicting of sin, and it could only do this if it had the status of a covenant with the power of life and death. Sinai was indeed the *handmaid* of the gospel of grace but it must not be confused with the gospel of grace itself. And it must also be seen that it cannot perform the handmaid function of preparation unless it has the power of life and death.

John Owen, the greatest theologian among the English Puritans, is the exception to most writers. He saw clearly that the Ten Commandments constituted a legal covenant that was totally devoid of grace. He is one of the few writers (John Bunyan is another one) that knew how to separate law and grace. The following quotation is Owen's explanation of the meaning of the word "law." It is taken from a sermon on Rom. 6:14 entitled "You are not under the law, but under grace:"

> The law is taken two ways:—1. For the **whole revelation of God in the Old Testament. In this sense it had grace in it, and so did give both life, and light, and strength against sin, as the Psalmist declares, Ps. 19:7-9. In this sense it contained not only the law of precepts, but the promise also and strength unto the church. In this sense it is not spoken of here, nor is anywhere opposed to grace.** 2. For the covenant rule of perfect obedience: "Do this, and live." In this sense men are said to be "under it," in opposition unto being "**under grace.**" They are under its power, rule, conditions, and authority, as a **covenant.**[7]

Owen believed that while grace can be found in the Old Testament *Scriptures,* there was no grace in the Old *Covenant*

---

[7]The Works of John Owen, Banner of Truth, Vol 7, P 542

because it was a legal/works covenant. The Tablets of the
Covenant said, "Do and live, disobey and die without mercy"
(Heb. 10:28). Israel was "under the law" as a covenant of life
and death in the sense of Owen's second definition of "the
law." He calls it "The **covenant rule** of perfect obedience."
Owen is following Paul when he shows the clear contrast between the covenant given to Israel and the covenant given to
the Church. This comes out clear in the last two sentences
of the above quotation. Israel was "under law" as opposed to
"under grace." They were under the Tablets of Stone as a
covenant, and that means, as Owen shows, that they were
"under its power, rule, conditions, and authority, as a **covenant**."

Owen boldly states that there was not an ounce of grace
in the law when it is viewed as the legal covenant given to the
nation of Israel at Sinai:

> *Fourthly,* **Christ is not in the Law;** he is not pro-
> posed in it, not communicated by it,—we are not made
> partakers of him thereby. This is the work of grace,
> of the gospel. In it is Christ revealed; by it he is pro-
> posed and exhibited unto us. . . . "[8]

If this statement either shocks or confuses us, we have not
yet understood the Biblical doctrine of law and grace. We have
not understood the nature, and function of the Ten Commandments. We have failed to see that the Tablets of Stone
were given to Israel as a ministration of death. They were meant
to push men to faith in the Gospel preached to Abraham. However, neither Christ nor the Gospel are found in the terms of
"Do and live, disobey and die." And these were the specific
covenant terms set forth at Sinai on the Tablets of Stone. It
was their terms that Israel pledged themselves to obey. It was
these disobedience to these covenant terms that caused their
captivities.

---

[8]Owen, p 551

We must emphasize the gracious act of God in *physically* redeeming Israel out of Egypt and, at the same time, not neglect the fact that God immediately put Israel under a *conditional legal* covenant at Sinai. Especially when this is so clear in the Scripture. Notice how clearly the following texts of Scripture show this truth in the "if" and "then" nature of this conditional covenant:

> *Ye have seen what I did unto the Egyptians, and how I bare you on eagles' wings, and brought you unto myself. Now therefore, **IF ye will obey** my voice indeed, and **keep my covenant, THEN ye shall be** a peculiar treasure unto me above all people: for all the earth is mine: and ye shall be unto me a kingdom of priests, and an holy nation. These are the words which thou shalt speak unto the children of Israel.*
>
> Ex. 19:4-6

It seems impossible to make the "if/then" relationship in this text to be anything other than a legal covenant promising certain blessings as a reward for obeying the covenant. The special nationhood status of Israel was based on the Ten Commandments as a covenant. This covenant was conditional because it a was legal/works covenant that promised life and threatened death. Israel failed to earn the blessings promised in the covenant. But under the New Covenant, the Church becomes the Israel of God and all her members are kings and priests (a kingdom of priests). Christ, as our covenant Surety (Heb. 7:22), has kept the Old Covenant for us and earned every blessing it promised.

Even a cursory comparison of Ex. 19:5,6 with I Pet. 2:9 will show that both texts use the identical words.[9] Ex. 19 gives

---

[9]We have worked this point out in great detail in a forth coming book entitled *The Four Seeds of Abraham.* This book examines the basic presuppositions of both Dispensationalism and Covenant Theology as they both relate to the promise of God made to Abraham and his seed." It will be available from Crowne Publications, P.O. Box 688, Southbridge, Mass., 01550

a list of the specific blessings that were promised IF Israel would
keep the covenant (the Ten Commandments). Israel never
obeyed the terms of the covenant and therefore never received
these blessings. She was finally cast off and lost her special
national privileges. I Pet. 2:9 shows the Church inheriting those
very blessings only because Christ has kept of the Old Covenant
for us. Notice the word for word comparison of Ex. and I Pet.:

Now therefore, IF ye will *obey my voice indeed, and*	But you *are*
keep my covenant, THEN ye shall be	[because Christ the covenant for us]
(1) a **peculiar treasure** unto me above all people: for all the earth is mine: and ye shall be unto me	(1) a **chosen people,** . . . a people belonging to God
(2) a **kingdom of priests**, and a	(2) a **royal [kingly] priesthood,**
(3) **holy nation.**	(3) a **holy nation,**
Ex. 19:4-6	**I Peter 2:9**

> **Both the beginning and the ending of Israel's spe-
> cial national standing and privileges are connected
> with their keeping or breaking the Ten Command-
> ments, or covenant.**

The passage quoted above (Ex. 19:5,6) certainly proves this
point as to the founding of the nation. The ending of Israel's
special national status proves the same thing. Israel's special
national standing and privileges ended *when the covenant
ended that had established them as a nation.* The most important verse in the NT Scriptures from either a dispensational
or covenantal point of view is Mt. 27:51. The New Covenant
was ratified by the blood of Christ the moment Christ died
on the cross. At that instant the veil of the temple was rent
from top to bottom by the finger of God. The way into the

Most Holy place is now open to all believers twenty four hours a day. The same God that wrote that first covenant in stone with His finger now writes the new message with the same fingers as he tears the veil and opens up His immediate presence to "all who come." The First Covenant said, *"Do not come near* or even touch this mountain or you die," but the New Covenant that takes its place says, *Come and welcome,* the door is wide open." It was the change of covenants that makes the difference in the following texts:

*The Lord said to Moses, "Tell your brother Aaron **not** to come whenever he chooses into the **Most Holy Place** behind the curtain in front of the atonement cover on the ark, or else he will die. . . . " Lev. 17:2*	*Therefore, brothers, since we have confidence to enter the **Most Holy Place** by the blood of Jesus, by a **new and living way** . . . Let us come boldly. . . . Heb. 10:19*

At the very moment that the veil was rent, Israel's national status and privileges were ended[10] and everything that was connected to that special covenant relationship was also ended. The minsitry of Aaron was finished, the sacrifices were fulfilled, the Tabernacle was no longer "holy," and the Tables of the Covenant (Ten Commandments) in the Ark of the Covenant were no longer in force as the covenant foundation of God's relationship to His people. A "better covenant" that was based on "better promises" (Heb. 8:6) has taken the place of the Tablets of Stone. The "moment" described by Matthew is the exact moment that the decisive historical shift from the Old Covenant to the New Covenant took place.

> *And when Jesus cried out again with a loud voice, he gave up the spirit. **At that moment** the curtain of the*

---

[10]We believe the Scripture makes a clear distinction between Israel as a "nation" and Israel as an "ethnic people." The first is finished but the second is not. For a clear presentation of ethnic Israel's hope for the future, see Romans, by John Murray, Vol II, pps XIV, XV.

temple was torn in two from top to bottom. The earth
shook and the rocks split.

Mt. 27:50,51 NIV

First century Jewery could not accept the total change of
status brought into being by the change of covenants. They
wanted to hang on to everything that was distinctive of the
Old. This explains their rejection of Christ as the Messiah. The
Jewish nation not only rejected the message spoken by Christ,
they totally dismissed one of the greatest objects lessons that
God ever gave. We do not know if they sewed that old veil
back together or made a new one, but regardless, in rehang-
ing that veil they disavowed every promise and earned every
judgment that their own prophets had clearly foretold. The
times of the Messiah and the Gospel blessing to *all people* that
had been promised in the Abrahamic covenant had finally
come. However, the Jewish nation could not accept this truth.
"There is *no difference*" could not penetrate the blind eyes
and proud heart of the bigoted Jew.

The rending of the veil not only raised the believing Gentile up to be on an equal basis with a believing Jew as a member of the Body of Christ, it also lowered the status of the
unbelieving Jew and put him on the same level as the Gentile
"dog." The Holy Place was not the only thing that was finished; there was no longer a Court of Gentiles. The heart of
this truth is set forth by Paul in Romans 9:1-11; Eph. 2:11-
21; Gal. 3:19-4-7; and Rom. 2 & 3.

**The Ten Commandments, or Tablets of Stone, con-
stituted the actual covenant document that established Israel as a Nation.**

Many things were added to the Tablets of Stone that explained and applied the covenant. Exodus chapters 20-22 is
called the "Book of the Covenant." The "Law of Moses" included everything in the Pentateuch, and as such, was sometimes called "the Law" or "the Covenant." However, the Tablets
of Stone, or Ten Commandments, were the specific covenant

document that established Israel's nationhood in the same sense that the Constitution of the USA is the covenant document that established the USA as a nation. The acts of Congress, the decisions of the Supreme Court, the rules of the IRS, Food and Health department laws, etc., are all part of the "law of the USA" just as the judicial, ceremonial, social and health laws are all part of the "law of Moses." However, the Constitution is still the specific and separate document upon which all else rests. The same is true of the Tablets of the Covenant, or Ten Commandments.

All of the laws of the various departments in our government grow out of the Constitution. They define and apply specific sections of the Constitution to given situations today. However, the fact remains that the actual **covenant document** upon which our nationhood was established and by which we are still governed, is the Constitution. In the same sense, the Ten Commandments written on the Tablets of Stone were the "words of the covenant" that constituted the basic **covenant foundation** of Israel's special nationhood before God. A chart of comparison may help us to understand this point:

Foundational Covenant Document of Israel nationhood	Foundational Covenant Document U.S.A. as a nation
Ten Commandments	The Constitution
General Laws	Congress
Judicial Laws	Supreme Court
Civil and Social Laws	Justice Department
Health Laws	Dept. of Health
Tithing Laws	Dept. of I.R.S.
"The Law of Moses"	"The Law of the USA."

CHAPTER 5

The Ten Commandments Were Given Only To the Nation Of Israel

The Old Testament Scriptures always state that the covenant written on the Tablets of Stone was made only with Israel at Sinai. We saw this truth in chapter one. We looked at the first time the words "Ten Commandments" were used in the Bible. This same text states that the Ten Commandments, as the covenant document, was given only to the nation of Israel:

> *And the LORD said unto Moses, Write thou these words: for after the **tenor of these words** I have made a **covenant** with thee and WITH ISRAEL. And he was there with the LORD forty days and forty nights; he did neither eat bread, nor drink water. And he wrote upon the tables the **words of the covenant, the ten commandments.***
>
> Ex. 34:27,28

When Moses refreshed Israel's mind concerning their covenant relationship with God, he specifically says that the covenant (Ten Commandments) was given at Horeb. This is clear in the following text:

> *The Lord our God made a covenant [Remember the covenant is the **Ten Commandments** or **Tablets of***

Stone] with us at Horeb. The Lord did not make this covenant with our fathers, but with us, with all of us alive here today.

Deut. 5:2,3

Moses insists that the covenant was "**not** made with our fathers," meaning the patriarchs,[11] but with the people that came out of Egypt. He then repeats the words of the covenant, or Ten Commandments, that were written on the Tablets of Stone.

The Prophets saw the coming of a New Covenant and spoke of it in glowing terms. Whenever they contrasted the Old Covenant with the New Covenant, they always state *when* and *with whom* the Old Covenant was made. Notice this in a classic passage in Jeremiah:

*Behold days are coming, declares the Lord, when I will make a **new covenant** with the house of Israel . . . , not like the **covenant** which I made with their fathers in the day I took them by the hands **to bring them out of the land** of Egypt. . . . "*

Jer. 31:31,32.

Notice the following things clearly set forth in this passage:

1. There was going to be a New Covenant. *"I will make a **new covenant**."*
2. The New Covenant was going to be *different in nature* from the Old Covenant. *"**Not like the covenant I** made with their *fathers"*
3. The Old Covenant being replaced was made at Sinai and made only with Israel. *"Made with their fathers **in the day** I took them by the hand to bring them out of **the land of Egypt"***

---

[11]The writer of Hebrews, as well as the prophecy in Jer. 31:33, established beyond question that the "fathers" referred to in this passage are the patriarchs. To make the statement refer to the immediate fathers of the people to whom Moses is speaking would involve a contradiction. It was specifically to these very "fathers" that God gave the covenant at Sinai.

How is it possible to read these words in Jeremiah and say, "God was not actually promising to make a new and different covenant with Israel. He was really promising a new *administration* of the *same covenant* they were already under?" It seems to us that such statements are literally contradicting what Jeremiah said. The rest of the Bible always says the same thing that Jeremiah said when it speaks on this subject. The following passage from I Kings appears to be going out of its way to affirm the facts we are setting forth:

> *There was nothing in the ark save the two **tables of stone,** which Moses put there **at Horeb, WHEN** the LORD **made a covenant** with the **children of Israel, WHEN they came out of the land of Egypt.***
>
> I Kings 8:9

The phrases "Tables of Stone," "Moses at Horeb," "made a covenant" and "children of Israel," in this text are the same key ingredients that we always find connected with the Ten Commandments. This passage of Scripture uses the word "when" two times. We could put a period after "children of Israel" and not lose the thought or argument. The last phrase in the sentence "When they came out of the land of Egypt" is almost redundant. The Holy Spirit must have wanted to impress this point on our minds.

The NT Scriptures always connect the Old Covenant with Israel.

Heb. 8:6-9 is the Apostolic interpretation of Jer. 31:31,32. The author of Hebrews clearly states: (1) *when* the Old Covenant was made; (2) *with whom* the Old Covenant was made; (3) the fact the New Covenant would be *different* than the Old Covenant. The passage is clear:

> . . . .*the time is coming, declares the Lord, when I will make a **new covenant** with the **house of Israel.** . . . It will **not be** like the covenant **I made with their forefathers** when **I took them by** the hand to lead them*

out Egypt. . . .

Heb. 8:7,8

It is not possible to make this verse promise a new *administration* of the same covenant. Nor is it possible to relate this covenant back to Adam in the garden. Neither the words of the prophecy in Jer. 31:33 nor the Apostolic interpretation in Heb. 8:7,8 will allow such an idea.

> **"Having the law"** as a covenant and the Gospel as a promise as opposed to **"not having the law"** and being without covenant or hope was the great difference **between the nation of Israel and the Gentiles** (Eph. 2:11-21).

The following text is a key passage on this particular point:

> *For when the Gentiles, **which have not the law**, do by nature the things contained in the law, these, **having not the law**, are a law unto themselves: Which show the **work of the law** written in their hearts, their **conscience** also bearing witness. . . .*

Rom. 2:14.

First of all, the word "law" in this passage clearly refers to the Tablets of Stone. It cannot refer to "a sense of moral duty" since all men have that by virtue of being God's image bearers. Paul is talking about a law that all men definitely *do not have*. If all men have "the law" in the sense that Paul is using the word in this passage, his argument does not make sense. He is contradicting himself in the same breath. Paul's whole point in the context of this passage is to show that the Jews are more guilty than the Gentiles. The basis of his proof is that the Gentiles *"without the law"* live better lives than the Jews do *"with* the law." The Jews alone have the special gift of the Law. And the specific law that he is talking about is the law written on the Tablets of Stone as a covenant.

Rom. 2:14 is not talking about a so called "ceremonial law."

Whatever the "law" is in this passage, it convicts the conscience of sin. Conscience, by nature and without special revelation, cannot convict men of disobedience to "ceremonial" laws. One of the many proofs that the Sabbath is not a "moral law" is the fact that we have never discovered a single instance of anyone knowing, by nature, the Sabbath law. This particular law must always be taught as special revelation just as it was to Israel at Sinai.[12] Gentiles intuitively knew that adultery was wrong but they never know intuitively that the seventh day is to be kept holy.

Most people misquote this passage of Scripture. Paul does not say, "The law" is written in the Gentile's heart. He says that certain behavior proves that there is a conviction of right and wrong in all men. This fact shows that conscience is alive and well even in the Gentiles. In fact, it is more alive and well in them than it is in the Jew. This power of conscience "shows the *work* of the law written in their hearts." The "work" of the law is to accuse or excuse according to the standard given to it. It condemns all violations of known wrong and rewards obedience to what is known to be right. All men have a conscience and they all experience, to a greater or lesser degree, conviction they have done wrong.

The Gentiles did *not* have "the law" but they *did have* the "work of the law" in their hearts. The law can only "work" true repentance that leads to faith if there is (1) a covenant with clear terms and (2) the individual has a knowledge of those terms. In giving Israel the law as a covenant, God enlightened the mind and sharpened the conscience. He sandwiched conscience under the Old Covenant and its threat of judgement. This caused a very painful death to all hope of eternal life in

---

[12]John Bunyan wrote an excellent article proving the Seventh Day Sabbath could not possibly be a so called "Creation Ordinance." To our knowledge, no one has attempted to answer his arguments. See, "Questions about the Nature and Perpetuity of the Seventh-Day Sabbath," by John Bunyan, The Works of John Bunyan, Vol. II, pp 359-387, Baker Book House. Also, Is Sunday the Christian Sabbath?, by Dr Robert Morey.

those who truly experienced the end for which the law covenant was given, namely, genuine "conviction of guilt." The same law actually "blinded" the rest of the Jews and made them worse off spiritually than the Gentiles.

We say again, it was most *gracious* of God to kill Israel's hope in their own efforts. However, it took a covenant of pure law with the power of life and death to do the job. There was not an ounce of grace in the Tablets of Stone but it was most gracious of God to give them to Israel as a covenant that could prepare the heart to receive grace!

Regardless of whether the reader agrees or disagree with what has just been said, one thing is certain. We cannot change a passage that emphatically states that Israel *had* a specific law that the Gentiles *did not* have into a text that says "all men have the same law." This is to destroy the text. Paul can only be referring to the Tables of Stone as a covenant.

It both amazes and amuses us to watch people waver back and forth when they cannot fit clear passages of Scripture into their theological system. They usually want to "eat their cake and have it too." If they are discussing the "unchanging moral law," they will insist that "the moral law (Ten Commandments) is written on ever man's heart." However, if they are discussing the canon of conduct for believer's today, these same people will insist that in regeneration "the moral law" (Ten Commandments) is written on the heart" by the Holy Spirit. In both cases it is said to be the *same law* that Scriptures clearly state was given *only* to the nation of Israel at Sinai on the Tablets of Stone.

Something seems to be a bit out of focus when all of this is put together. (1) If the first point is true, and the same law that was given to Israel at Sinai (the Ten Commandments) is indeed written on every man's heart, it is impossible to say the Gentiles are "without the law." They cannot be "without" the very law that is written "in" them. (2) If the second point, affirming that the same law written in the heathen, and given to Israel at Sinai, is also written on the heart of believer in regeneration, is true, there appears to be a contradiction. What need is there to write something on the heart that is already there? (3) If, in regeneration, the Holy Spirit writes the Ten Commandments on the heart of every believer, what then is the necessity of preaching those commandments to the Christian?

We must distinguish between the Ten Commandments as the terms of a legal covenant and the duties commanded by the individual commandments. The moment we do this a lot of confusion disappears and some difficult passages of Scripture become clear and simple. We will illustrate this point with one passage of Scripture. This passage in its context is pivotal to any correct understanding of the change of covenants:

> *But the ministry Jesus has received is as superior to theirs as the covenant of which he is mediator is superior to the old one, and it is founded on better promises.*
>
> *For if there had been nothing wrong with that first covenant, no place would have been sought for another. But God found fault with the people and said: "The time is coming, declares the Lord, when **I will make a new covenant** with the house of Israel and with the house of Judah. It will **not be like the covenant** I made with their forefathers when I took them by the hand to lead them out of Egypt, because they did not remain faithful to my covenant, and I turned away from them, declares the Lord. **This is the covenant I will make** with the house of Israel after that time, declares the Lord. **I will put my laws in their minds and write them on their hearts.** I will be their God, and they will be my people. No longer will a man teach his neighbor, or a man his brother, saying, 'Know the Lord,' because they will all know me, from the least of them to the greatest. For I will forgive their wickedness and will remember their sins no more." By calling this covenant "new," he has made the first one obsolete; and what is obsolete and aging will soon disappear.*
>
> Heb. 8:6-13

We have already noted the three distinct contrasts in verse 6. We saw the following: (1) Christ has a better **ministry** than Aaron; (2) because Christ's ministry is based on a new and *better* **covenant**; (3) the covenant Christ administers is superior to the covenant under which Aaron ministered because it is based on *better* **promises**.

Heb. 8:7-9 settles any discussion as to either *when* (at Sinai) or *with whom (Israel only) the Old Covenant was made. Heb. 8:11 shows that everyone, without a single exception, in the New Covenant community, or Church, "know the Lord." In other words, the text proves that the Church born under the New Covenant has a totally regenerate membership. We will now look at verse 10:*

> *This is the* **covenant** *I will make with the* **house of Israel** *after that time, declares the Lord. I will put my* **laws in their minds** *and write them on their hearts. I will be their God, and they will be my people.*
>
>   HEB. 8:10

The text emphasizes several important things. First, God promises to make a new covenant, and this covenant will be with the "house of Israel." We will not digress from the point under discussion except to say that the "house of Israel" in Heb. 8-10 must be the Church. The writer is not talking about the future but the present. This covenant cannot be pushed into a future millennium. Hebrews is talking about the priestly ministry of Christ over the Church. However, that is not our subject in this book.

The second major thing in the text is God's promise to put his laws in the mind and write them on the hearts of His New Covenant people. Now here is the question: *"What is the difference, if any, between the* **"covenant"** *and the word "laws" in this passage?"* Exactly what is God promising to do in this verse? Exactly what is the "New Covenant" He is making and precisely what "laws" is He going to write on the heart?

We should carefully note that God did not say, "In that

day I will give a new *administration* of the *same covenant* that
I gave Israel. I will write the old law of Sinai into the new heart
of the Christian." That is how some theologians read this passage. Likewise, the text does *not say*, "I will make a New
Covenant that destroys all of the Ten Commandments and al-
lows a believer to do as he pleases." That is how some liberals
view the text. No, the text, and its context, is talking about
both a new and better covenant than the old covenant at Sinai and the new experience of the law being written on the
heart by the indwelling Spirit.

The clear answers to the two questions that we asked lies
in understanding the three comparisons made in verse 6. Why
did the Old Covenant fail and thereby need to be replaced by
a new and better covenant? The answer is that it could not
secure the necessary obedience to its terms. It could not write
on the heart the desire to do the things that were written on
the Tablets of the Covenants. It could write on stone but not
on flesh (II Cor. 3). By nature all men hate God's authority
(Rom. 8:7) and even the mighty Law of God cannot change
that rebellion into a sincere desire to obey. The Old Covenant failed to bring sinners into God's presence because it could
not change the sinner's heart. It could not conquer sin in the
flesh nor it could cleanse the conscience from the guilt of sin.

Now listen carefully! The greater glory of the New Covenant is *not* that the standards or laws have been either lowered or done away. It is *not* that the moral duties demanded
on the Tables of Stone are no longer binding on a Christian.
No, No, that is to miss the whole point. The greater glory of
the New Covenant is that *no obedience at all is required as
the terms of being saved simply* because the very terms of the
Tablets of the Covenant have been *finally and fully met in
the Person and work of Surety,* the Lord Jesus Christ. The
glory of the New Covenant is in the words, "IT IS FINISHED."
Paul states the glory of the New Covenant in the classic passage in Rom. 4:5:

However, to the man who does not work but trusts
God who justifies the wicked, his faith is credited as
righteousness.

Rom. 4:5

This is the "rest" that weary souls enter into when they
come under the yoke of Christ and are liberated from the yoke
of the covenant given to Moses on Sinai. We doubt not that
our Lord Jesus had this very contrast in mind when He gave
that great gospel invitation in Matthew 11:

*Come to **me**, all you who are weary and burdened,*
*and **I will give you rest**. Take **my yoke** upon you*
*and **learn from me, for I am gentle and humble in***
heart, and you will find rest for your souls**. For **my
***yoke** is easy and my burden is light."*

Matt. 11:28-30

Every thing in that passage is a contrast with Moses and
the old law covenant. The yoke of the covenant written on
the Tables of Stone was a burden impossible to bear. The yoke
written in the blood of Calvary is a privilege and delight to
bear. The New Covenant is nothing less than Christ Himself
and His finished work. When God said, "I will make a new
covenant," He was saying, "I will give you Christ to be your
covenant Keeper. He will both keep the law and die under
its curse." The message has now become "It is finished" instead of "Do or Die." The New Covenant is grace and not
works.

What then are the "laws" spoken of in Heb. 8:10? Exactly
what "laws" does the Holy Spirit write on the heart of a New
Covenant believer? These laws, as far as their *content*, are basically the very same moral laws that were written on the tables
of stone. Heb 8:10 is not talking about two different "sets"
of laws that totally contradict each other as if there were two
"kinds of morality." The morality of the New Covenant does
not destroy the true morality demanded in the laws of the Old

Covenant. It takes that morality to a higher level. It is true that Christ adds laws that were impossible for Moses to ever give but that does not mean Christ contradicts Moses.[13] Hebrews is talking about two different motivations that grow out of two different kinds of *covenants.*"   II Cor. 3 is the Holy Spirit's commentary on Heb. 8:10. Neither of these passages are teaching that God "tatoos" the exact words of the Decalogue on our hearts. Both passages are talking about the powerful effect of regeneration that results in a totally new and different attitude toward God. These two passages are picturing the removal of the stony heart that hated the Tablets of Stones and all they represented. It is describing the effect of regeneration in replacing the stony heart with a heart of flesh. The new heart of flesh loves **all** of God's revealed laws, not just a one small code, simply because it loves the new Lawgiver Who teaches us those laws.

The difference is not in the specific duties demanded but the difference between law and grace as covenants. It is the difference, in some cases, of the *identical duties* being enforced from *without* by fear and force, in the case of the Old Covenant, and being constrained by love from within a heart rejoicing in a covenant of grace. These two passages are talking about the difference between the conscience being under the old Pedagogue, the Tables of Stone, and being under the new Pedagogue, the indwelling Holy Spirit.

---

[13]We have worked this out in a book entitled "But I Say Unto You." This book shows that Christ supercedes and replaces Moses as the New Lawgiver. Christ changes some of the laws of Moses; raises some others to a higher level; discards some others altogether; and adds some laws that are totally new. However, this is not contradicting Moses as if he were wrong. The book is available from Crowne Publications, P.O. Box 688, Southbridge, Mass., 01550.

CHAPTER 6

The Seventh Day Sabbath Was the Sign Of the Mosaic Covenant!

B ecause the Tablets of Stone were a distinct covenant, they were accompanied with a specific "covenant sign." We are aware that very few writers or preachers ever think of the Sabbath as the sign of the covenant written on the Tablets of Stone. However, this is not because the Word of God is not both clear and emphatic on this point. One of the questions that is nearly always asked when the Sabbath is discussed goes something like this:

"If the Sabbath was not part of the 'moral law,' then why was it included on the Tablets of Stone as one of the Ten Commandments?"

We could only wish that every question that we are asked was as easy to answer as this one. The Sabbath was the *sign of the covenant and therefore it had to be* part of the covenant document of which it *was the sign.* The answer is just that simple.

The following texts not only show us that the Sabbath was the sign of the covenant given at Sinai, they also show the great importance of the Sabbath sign:

*And the LORD spake unto Moses, saying, Speak thou also unto the children of Israel, saying, Verily **my sab-***

*baths ye shall keep: for it is a **sign between me and you** throughout your generations; that ye may know that I am the LORD that doth sanctify you. Ye shall keep the sabbath therefore; for it is holy unto you: every one that defileth it shall surely be put to death: for whosoever doeth any work therein, that soul shall be cut off from among his people. Six days may work be done; but in the seventh is the sabbath of rest, holy to the LORD: whosoever doeth any work in the sabbath day, he shall surely be put to death. Wherefore the **children of Israel** shall keep **the sabbath,** to observe the sabbath throughout their generations, for a **perpetual covenant.** It is a **sign between me and the children of Israel for ever:** for in six days the LORD made heaven and earth, and on the seventh day he rested, and was refreshed. And he gave unto Moses, when he had made an end of communing with him upon mount Sinai, **two tables** of testimony, tables of stone, written with the finger of **God.***

Ex. 31:12-18

This passage establishes these facts:

1. The Ten Commandments are synonymous with "Tables of Stone" and the two "tables of testimony" in this passage. They are the actual covenant document that established Israel's special national status with God. *"two tables of testimony, tables of stone, written with the finger of God."*

2. The Sabbath, or Fourth Commandment, was the sign of the covenant. *"the children of Israel shall keep the **Sabbath . . .** for a perpetual **covenant.** It is a **sign** between me and the children of Israel forever."*

3. The sign of the covenant, or Sabbath, stands for the whole covenant. To break the sign is to despise the entire covenant. *"keep the Sabbath . . . for a perpetual **covenant."***

4. The covenant was made only with the nation of Israel." . . . *the **children of Israel** shall keep the Sabbath. . . . It is a **sign** between me and the **children of Israel**. . . . "*

5. The essence of the Sabbath commandment was to refrain from all physical work. *"whosoever doeth **any work**. . . . Six days may **work be done**, but the seventh is the **sabbath of rest** . . . whosoever doeth **any work** in the sabbath day, he shall surely be put to death."*

The following passage from Ezekiel is helpful at this point. It not only shows that the Sabbath was the sign of the covenant written on the Tables of Stone, it also shows that this particular commandment was so important only because it was the covenant's sign. Read the text carefully:

*And I gave them my statutes, and shewed them my judgments, which if a man **DO**, he shall even **live in them**. Moreover also I gave them **my sabbaths,** to be a sign between me and them, that they might know that I am the LORD that sanctify them. But the house of Israel rebelled against me in the wilderness: they walked not in my statutes, and they despised my judgments, which if a man do, he shall even live in them; and **my sabbaths** they greatly polluted: **THEN** I said, I would pour out my fury upon them in the wilderness, to consume them. But I wrought for my name's sake, that it should not be polluted before the heathen, in whose sight I brought them out. Yet also I lifted up my hand unto them in the wilderness, that I would not bring them into the land which I had given them, flowing with milk and honey, which is the glory of all lands; Because they despised my judgments, and walked not in my statutes, but polluted **my SABBATHS:** for their heart went after their idols. Nevertheless mine eye spared them from destroying them, neither did I make an end of them in the wilderness. But I said unto their*

children in the wilderness, Walk ye not in the statutes
of your fathers, neither observe their judgments, nor
defile yourselves with their idols: I am the LORD your
God; walk in my statutes, and keep my judgments, and
*do them; And **hallow my SABBATHS;** and they shall*
*be a **SIGN between me and you,** that ye may know*
that I am the LORD your God.

Ezek. 20:12-20

Notice the "then" in verse 13 and its connection to vs 16
and 20. Israel committed many and grievous sins but it was
not until they "profaned the sabbath" that they went into captivity. Again, this shows that breaking the "sign" of the covenant
was the same as despising the whole covenant. Profaning the
Sabbath was the worst possible sin that an Israelite could commit. One of Israel's captivities was measured in terms of how
many years they had refused to observe the sabbath year law
and leave the land lay idle (Cf Jer. 29:10 and II Chron. 36:21).
It is obvious that the most important of the Ten Commandments, as far as it involved judgment, was the fourth and its
importance lay solely in the fact that it was the sign of the
covenant. The fact that the judgment of captivity for seventy
years was for breaking the Sabbath *year law* shows that all
of the Sabbaths were just as holy as the Seventh Day Sabbath. Perhaps it would be well to look at a few passages that
demonstrate the importance of a covenant's sign. It will help
us to understand the apparent "out of proportion" punish-
ment in several instances.

Why was picking up some sticks a capital offense?

For a long time we pondered the awful severity of God's
judgment on a man for merely picking up some sticks. It was
not until we understood the things we are discussing in this
book that we realized what a horrible sin the man had committed. Here is the passage:

*And while the children of Israel were in the wilderness, they found a man that **gathered sticks upon the sabbath day**. And they that found him gathering sticks brought him unto Moses and Aaron, and unto all the congregation. And they put him in ward, because it was not declared what should be done to him. And the Lord said unto Moses, the man shall be surely **put to death:** all the congregation shall stone him with stones without the camp. And all the congregation brought him without the camp, and **stoned him with stones, and he died;** as the Lord commanded Moses.*

Num. 15:32-36

This was not a "tough on the first case as an example to others" action by God. Picking up sticks was one of the worst possible sins that the man could commit under the Old Covenant because he was breaking the "sign" of the covenant and thereby disavowing the entire covenant. The Sabbath was to Israel's relationship with God exactly what a wedding ring is to a marriage relationship. They are both visible signs of a covenant. The ring is a "sign" of the obligation to keep the covenant vows just taken in the ceremony. To take off the ring, throw it at the other person, and walk away would be to deny the entire marriage relationship. This is exactly what Sabbath breaking was under the Old Covenant since it was the sign of that covenant. Breaking the Sabbath disannulled the whole covenant relationship with God. Profaning the Sabbath was denying all of the vows taken at Mt. Sinai. It was the same as deliberately spitting in God's face and then, in defiant self-sufficiency and rebellion, walking away and doing some physical work.

A comparison of the Mosaic covenant with other covenants shows that the seventh day Sabbath was the sign of the Mosaic covenant.

Every major covenant will always have a covenant sign.

When we compare the language used in the Bible in the establishment of several covenants, it shows us that the Ten Commandments were a distinct and separate covenant. The texts also establish beyond question that the Sabbath was the sign of the covenant given to Israel at Sinai. Look at the following comparisons:

> Noahaic covenant—" . . . *this is the **sign of the covenant** I have established. . . . "* Gen. 9:8-17 NIV

> Abrahamic covenant—*"This is my **covenant** . . . you are to undergo circumcision, and it will be a **sign of the covenant** between me and you.* Gen. 17:11 NIV

> Mosaic covenant—" . . . you must observe my Sabbaths. *This will be a **sign** between me and you for the generations to come. . . . The Israelites are to observe the **Sabbath** for the generations to come as a lasting covenant."* Ex. 31:12-18 NIV

We can no more deny that God made a separate covenant with Moses than we can deny that He made a separate covenant with Abraham. Likewise, we can no more deny that the Sabbath was the sign of covenant that was written on the Tables of Stone than we can deny that the rainbow is the sign of the covenant made with Noah or circumcision the sign of the Abrahamic covenant.

A comparison of the two different reasons for keeping the Sabbath day holy helps us to understand the purpose of the "sign" of the covenant.

The phrase "as the Lord thy God commanded thee" following the commandment to keep the seventh day holy is found in Dt. 5:12 but the same phrase is not found in Ex. 20:8. It is obvious why it is not the other way around. This phrase in Dt. 5:12 cannot possibly be referring back to Creation. It has to refer to Ex. 20:8 since this commandment was not given until Sinai. God did not "command" Adam to keep the Sabbath but He did, at Mt. Sinai, command Israel to keep the Sabbath as the sign of the covenant that He had just made with them. Another reason that it is impossible to make the statement "as the Lord thy God commanded thee" in Dt. 5:12 refer back to Genesis is the specific reason this particular version of the Ten Commandments gives for keeping the Sabbath. Dt. 5:15 does not even mention God resting at Creation. It specifically gives the redemption from Egypt as the reason that Israel was to "remember the Sabbath." How could God possibly have given a commandment in the Garden of Eden to remember Israel's deliverance from Egypt? Imagine either Adam or Abraham being commanded to "Remember the Sabbath day because I delivered you from bondage in Egypt." It would not have made a bit of sense.

What do we "remember" at the Lord's Table?

What should we see emphasized in the words our Lord gave us when He instituted the remembrance sign and service of the New Covenant? How should we feel when we read or hear the following words:

> *In the same way, after supper he took the cup, saying, "This cup is the **new covenant** in my blood; do this, whenever you drink it, in **remembrance of me.**" For whenever you eat this bread and drink this cup, you **proclaim the Lord's death** until he comes.* I Cor. 11:25-26

What should we feel as we "remember" the truth symbolized in the emblems (bread and wine) of the remembrance service celebrating the New Covenant? It would seem that our hearts should feel the liberty and joy of assurance of forgiveness. A feeling of either bondage or fear have no rightful place in our hearts as we rejoice in the memory of the death of our Lord Jesus Christ for our sins. When we remember His promise to come again, hope and joy should fill our minds and emotions.

What a different feeling we would get if we were 7th Day
Adventists and "remembered" the reason for our worshipping
on the Sabbath (Saturday) instead of the Lord's Day? We would
think of God our Creator and Law Giver and the law covenant
written on the Tablets of the Covenant. Our meeting on Saturday (the Sabbath) would be honoring the sign of the covenant
under which we were worshipping. We would remind ourselves
of the just covenant claims that God demanded of us. The
Tablets of Stone would still be the written code against us because of our sin. As our minds went back to the Old Covenant (Ten Commandments), we would smell the smoke from
Sinai and hear its terrible thunder and roar. However, this is
the *exact experience* that Sinai was *supposed to produce* in
the conscience of those who were under it as a covenant! This
was the stated purpose for which God gave that law in the first
place. And the purpose of the Sabbath sign was to remind of
those covenant terms. And the Scripture no where changes
the nature and function of either the covenant or its sign.

The God designed function of the Tables of Stone, or Ten
Commandments was conviction and fear not joy and hope. The
same moral rules that furnish our minds with help in pleasing
our heavenly Father functioned in the *conscience* of an Israelite as the condemning *covenant of life and death* (II Cor.
3:6-18) of their covenant God. However, we must remember
that this was God's declared intention in giving the Tablets
of Stone in the first place. Perhaps a chart comparing the remembrance signs and services of the two covenants will help
make clear what we are saying:

Old Covenant	New Covenant
Points to Creation	Points to Calvary
Emphasizes Lawgiver and Judge	Emphasizes Christ as Redeemer
This (keep Sabbath) do . . .	"THIS (remember My death) do . . .
in remembrance" of your duty.	in remembrance of ME."

The moment we see the clear contrast that Christ is making when instituting the remembrance service for celebrating the New Covenant, everything falls into place. When Jesus said "THIS do in remembrance of ME" He was contrasting the New Covenant, and its remembrance sign, with the Old Covenant, and its remembrance sign. He was saying, "Instead of keeping the Sabbath in remembrance of the old creation and Israel's redemption, THIS do in remembrance of Me and the deliverance I have accomplished."

The Old Covenant bound men to God as their Creator and Lawgiver and celebrated the work of the old creation. The New Covenant binds us to God as our Redeemer through our Lord Jesus Christ and celebrates the work of the new creation. The one reminds us of sin and the other reminds of forgiveness. Read I Cor. 11:25-27 and emphasize the word "this" and think of the contrast that Christ is making between the Old Covenant that He replaced and the New Covenant that He established.

CHAPTER 7

The Tablets Of Stone Were the Center Of Israel's Worship

Everything in Israel's life and worship revolved around the Tabernacle. The visible proof that God was among the nation was the cloud by day and the pillar of fire by night. God dwelt behind the veil in the Most Holy Place. That was the most important and Holy spot on the whole earth because God's immediate presence was there. Only the High Priest, on the yearly Day of Atonement, was allowed into God's presence in the Most Holy Place. Taking the blood, that had been shed on the altar, and sprinkling it on the Mercy Seat, or lid of the Ark of the Covenant, was Aaron's most important function of the whole year. As the Most Holy Place was the most holy spot on earth, so the Ark of the Covenant was the single most Holy piece of furniture. That box was important and Holy because of its contents. If we understand the purpose and function of the Tabernacle and its ministry around the Ark of the Covenant, we will automatically understand the purpose of the Ten Commandments. The two are identical and the function of the Tables of Stone never change in the Bible. The function did not "change." It ended! The purpose and function of the Tables of Stone never changed from the day of their inception at Mt. Sinai until the day that "written code" was nailed to the cross.

The "Ark of the Covenant" was so named because of its CONTENT.

We will review one point covered earlier concerning the
Ark. The Ark of the Covenant was built for the express purpose of housing the specific covenant document that established Israel as a nation and that covenant document was the
Ten Commandments. The Ark of the Covenant housed the
Ten Commandments. The Ten Commandments are the Old
Covenant. It was called the "Ark of the Covenant" and the
"Ark of Testimony" because it was the written covenant testimony against Israel when they disobeyed the covenant terms,
or Ten Commandments. All of this is so clear and so simple
when we use the terms and phrases used by the Holy Spirit.

Notice how the following texts establish what has just been
said:

> *And they shall make an ark of shittim wood: two cub-
> its and a half shall be the length thereof, and a cubit
> and a half the breadth thereof, and a cubit and a half
> the height thereof.*
>
> Ex. 25:10

> *And thou shalt put into the **ark the testimony** which
> I shall give thee.*
>
> Ex. 25:16

> *And he spread abroad the tent over the tabernacle, and
> put the covering of the tent above upon it;as the LORD
> commanded Moses. And he took and put the **testi-
> mony into the ark,** and set the staves on the ark, and
> put the mercy seat above upon the ark:*
>
> Ex. 40:19,20

It is obvious that the word "testimony" and the word
"covenant" are interchangeable in this verse. The Ark of the
"Testimony" is the Ark of the "Covenant." It is just as obvious, in the following passages, that the "Testimony" is the

Ten Commandments written on the Tablets of Stone:

> *At that time the LORD said unto me, Hew thee two tables of stone like unto the first, and come up unto me into the mount, and make thee an ark of wood. And I will write on the tables the words that were in the first tables which thou brakest, and thou shalt put them in the ark. And I made an ark of shittim wood, and hewed two tables of stone like unto the first, and went up into the mount, having the two tables in mine hand. And he* **wrote on the tables,** *according to the first writing, the* **ten commandments,** *which the LORD spake unto you in the mount out of the midst of the fire in the day of the assembly: and the LORD gave them unto me. And I turned myself and came down from the mount, and* **put the tables in the ark** *which I had made; and there they be, as the LORD commanded me.*
>
> Dt. 10:1-5

Why were the Ten Commandments placed in the Ark of the Covenant? Why was that box so sacred that humans hands were not even allowed to touch it. To see how Holy the Ark was, read II Sam. 5 & 6. When we understand why a man was instantly killed by God for merely putting his hand on the Ark to steady it, we will see the nature, purpose and function of the Ten Commandments inside the Ark of the Covenant.

There could be no entrance into the presence of God in the Most Holy Place as long as the Tablets of Stone in the Ark of the Covenant were in FORCE AS A COVENANT.

The nature, purpose, and function of the Ark of the Covenant is the nature, purpose and function of the Ten Commandments! The Ten Commandments began their ministry in the history of Redemption when they were placed in the box that was designed especially to be their home. And ex-

actly what was the purpose and function of the Ark of the
Covenant and its contents? What particular function did it play
in the life and worship of the nation of Israel?

The answer to this question is easy. The Ark of the
Covenant closed off all approach into the immediate presence
of God until the terms of the covenant spelled out on the
Tablets of Stone had been fully met. Those terms demanded
a kind of life that no sinner could produce. It was the failure
to obey the covenant terms that closed off the entrance into
God's presence. Aaron alone was allowed, one day a year, to
enter the Most Holy Place. He always had to take with him
some blood that had been shed on the altar of sacrifice. The
whole purpose and function of the Ten Commandments in the
Ark of the Covenant can be summed up in one word **DEATH**.
The message in the box was the same message on the veil.
In big letters it said **"KEEP AWAY — DO NOT EVEN
TOUCH!"** It was disobedience to this message that caused
Uzzah to die (II Sam. 6:6,7).

Paul is saying the same truth in the following passages:

> He has made us competent as ministers of a **new
> covenant**—not of the letter but of the Spirit; for the
> letter kills, but the Spirit gives life. Now if the **min-
> istry that brought death, which was engraved in
> letters on stone**. . . .
>
> II Cor. 3:6,7

> Once I was alive apart from law; but when the com-
> mandment came, sin sprang to life and **I died**. I found
> that the very commandment that was **intended to
> bring life** actually brought **death**. For sin, seizing the
> opportunity afforded by the commandment, deceived
> me, and through the **commandment put me to death**.
>
> Rom. 7:9,10

It is true that Paul said the "commandment was ordained
to *life*." However, because of sin, he discovered the commandment was "death to him." The Ten Commandments did in-

deed promise life to anyone that kept them perfectly. They also promised death to all who failed to keep them. However, the Tablets of Stone could not do either of these things if it did not have the status of a covenant. A bare commandment cannot kill unless the death penalty is connected to it. And no commandment can give life unless the commandment is the terms of a covenant that promises life. Paul specifically says, "the **very commandment** that was **intended to bring life."** It is obvious that he was talking about the Tablets of the Covenant, or Ten Commandments. Likewise Paul says, "the **commandment** put me to death." If the Ten Commandments, considered as a covenant, was not a legal/works covenant that promised life for obedience and death for disobedience then Paul's statements do not make sense.

Jesus responded to the rich young ruler as He did only because the Ten Commandments offers life to those who perfectly obey. The young man wanted to "earn" his way to eternal life and Jesus told him to "Keep the Law" (Mt. 19:17). When the young man asked, "Which one?", Jesus quoted 5 of the commandments written on the Tablets of the Covenant and threw in the "second greatest commandment of all" (Lev. 19:18) for good measure.

It is silly and contradictory to ask, "If a son of Adam perfectly kept the Ten Commandments, would he still not have his original sin?" The question states a contradiction. If the person perfectly kept the law it would prove that **he did not have original sin in the first place.** It is impossible for *any* son of Adam to obey the law perfectly simply because *every* son of Adam *has a sinful nature* inherited from his father Adam that keeps him from perfect obedience.

The second fact, that all men have a sinful nature, absolutely precludes the first situation, a son of Adam perfectly obeying the Ten Commandments, from ever being even a possibility. No sinner can earn righteousness by obeying the Tablets of Stone simply because no sinner can obey them. However, the Tablets of the Covenant still *offers life and righteousness* just

as surely as they *threaten death and damnation*. The problem
that prevents anyone from earning righteousness by keeping
the Old Covenant is in the nature of the sinner and not in
the nature of the covenant.

As long as the covenant in the Ark of the Covenant was
in force it closed off approach to God. It said, "Stay Away!"
No one could meet the terms of that covenant. The "words
of the covenant," or Ten Commandments, clearly demanded
perfect obedience. No one could give the perfect obedience
the covenant demanded and thereby earn the righteousness
that it promised. Once the covenant had been broken, a sacrifice must be offered to take away the curse of the broken
covenant. The entire ministry of the priesthood revolved around
the sins against that covenant in the Ark. The blood sprinkled on the Mercy Seat in the Most Holy Place made the Israelite *ceremonially* clean for *one year* but that blood could
not "cleanse the conscience" (Heb. 9:15; 10:2,22). Aaron could
neither present a Holy sinless life to the covenant nor could
he present a blood sacrifice that was sufficient to truly atone
and deliver from the curse of the broken covenant.

The whole purpose and function of Aaron's ministry was
a constant reminder of sin against the covenant in the Ark
of the Covenant. Everything was designed to remind people
of their sin. Those in whom the covenant wrought true repentance were given hope in a coming Deliverer. However,
even they had to live their day by day life under the threat
of the Old Covenant.

The Lord Jesus Christ, our Surety of the covenant, was
born under the very law covenant housed in the Ark of the
Covenant. He fulfilled everyone of its demands and earned the
righteousness that it promised. He then died under the curse
of that law covenant (Gal 3:14) and forever removed its curse
from His people. It was at the exact moment of His enduring
that covenant's curse unto death that the New Covenant was
established and the Old Covenant (the Ten Commandments),
and everything that attended it, was disannulled because it had

been fulfilled. The absolute proof of this was God renting the veil from top to bottom. The sign that said "Stay Out" was changed to "Enter Boldly." The change was possible because the terms of the Old Covenant have been fully met. The Tables of Stone have been done away and the New Covenant has been established forever in the blood and righteousness of Christ.

The priesthood, services, sacrifices etc., all started and ended at the same time as the Old Covenant that necessitated their being established.

It is not possible to understand the Biblical teaching on the change of covenants that is so clearly set forth in the Book of Hebrews until we see the particular truth we are discussing at the moment. This is the whole burden of Hebrews chapters 8-10. Notice one section:

> *Now the **first covenant** had regulations for worship (Don't confuse the actual covenant, the Ten Commandments, with all of the "regulations") and also an earthly sanctuary. A tabernacle was set up. In its first room were the lamp stand, the table and the consecrated bread; this was called the Holy Place. Behind the second curtain was a room called the Most Holy Place, which had the golden altar, and the gold covered **ark of the covenant.** This ark contained the jar of manna, Aaron's staff that had budded, and the **stone tables** of the **covenant** [Remember the Ten Commandments were written on those Tablets).*

> Heb. 9:1-4

The whole purpose for the priesthood and sacrificial system coming into existence was to administer the Old Covenant:

> *For this reason Christ is the mediator of a new covenant, that those who are called may receive the promised eternal inheritance—now that he has died as a ransom to set them free from the sins com-*

mitted under the first covenant.

Heb. 9:15

Everything pertaining to Israel's special national relationship to God, including the Tablets of the Covenant (Ten Commandments), ended when Christ, by His obedient life and
death, met every claim and demand of the Old Covenant written in stone. Deliverance from the just claims of that covenant
was necessary before the true Israel of God could be created
and established on the New Covenant. The setting "free from
the sins committed under the first covenant" is what required
Christ to be "born under the law" (Gal. 4:1-7). The Tables
of Stone are now as obsolete as both the Ark that housed
them and the priestly ministry that sprinkled animal blood
on the lid of the Ark.

The relationship of the Law Covenant (the stone tablets
in the Ark) to the Mercy Seat (the lid of the Ark) is one
of the clearest pictures of the Gospel in the OT Scriptures.
It also sets forth the Biblical relationship of law and grace.
The Tablets of the Covenant (Ten Commandments) in the
Ark represents the just demands of the law covenant. There
is the Law! The lid of the Ark covers the broken covenant
of law with the blood of atonement. There is the Gospel!
There is not an ounce of "grace" or "Gospel" in the law
covenant in the box. It is pure law demanding perfect obedience as the condition of blessing and death for disobedience. The blood on the Mercy Seat covers and hides the
broken covenant and the sins against that covenant. That
is grace! It was indeed very "gracious" of God to give the
law covenant to make know sin, and it was even more
gracious to provide a payment to cover the sin. But there
was no grace in the terms of the covenant in the box. John
Newton had it right. "It was Grace (using the law in the box)
that taught my heart to fear; And Grace (through the blood
on the Mercy Seat) **relieved that fear.**"

Some theologians will challenge the truth that the Ten
Commandments offered life and righteousness for perfect obe-

dience. They deny this Biblical fact only because their theology simply cannot acknowledge the validity of any kind of a covenant of *works* after Gen. 3:15. Our response to such a view is this: If the Ten Commandments are not a legal/works covenant that can award life and righteousness then *we as believers have no righteousness.* Our righteousness is an earned righteousness. It was earned by Christ keeping some law covenant that had the authority to award obedience with life and righteousness. What other law covenant, besides the covenant at Sinai, could Christ have possibly been "born under" to earn this righteousness for us? Did our "Surety of the Covenant" endure the curse of a covenant of grace or a legal covenant of works when died on the cross? Let the readers find the answers to these questions in their own theological system if they can.

Some writers try to make Galatians 3:24,25 and Col. 2:14 teach that Christ's blood atonement delivered us from the "bondage and rigors" of the ceremonial law. How can anyone believe that God the Father would put our Lord to death on the cross just so we could eat pork and avoid circumcision? The very idea is monstrous. Those who hold this view are attempting to prove that the "law" that was dismissed in Gal. 3:24,25 cannot possibly be referring to the Ten Commandments. That is not possible according their system of theology. This is another example of twisting a clear text in order to hang on to a theology that will not fit into the Scriptures.

The believer has constant and immediate access into the presence of God (Heb. 10:17-24) only because passages like Gal. 3:24,25 and Col. 2:14 do refer to the Tables of Stone. The law covenant has been dismissed as the Pedagogue over the conscience of God's people. The least saint under the New Covenant enjoys a privilege that even godly Aaron could not enjoy. The purpose and function of the Tables of the Covenant (Ten Commandments) *inside the Ark* are just as finished as the Ark that held them. The yoke on the con-

science that kept sinners from entering God's presence has
been removed through the "doing and dying" of our Substitute. We must never allow anyone to put that yoke back
on our conscience. We must see the law dismissed for ever
as a covenant. Its sword was wiped clean of our Substitute's
blood and forever sheathed that day at Golgotha.

Paul's appeal to the Galatians should be tattooed on our
mind and heart:

> *It is for freedom that Christ has set us free. Stand*
> *firm, then, and do not let yourselves be burdened*
> *again by a yoke of slavery.*
>
> Gal. 5:1

What yoke is Paul talking about? It is clearly a reference
to "law," but to what specific law? The defenders of Moses
will immediately say, "Paul is talking about the ceremonial
law. That is the law that was dismissed and the yoke from
which we are set free. He could not possibly be talking about
the Ten Commandments." We would ask a few question of
such a view. How can the "ceremonial" law be such a terrible yoke of bondage? Our Lord lived His whole life under
every ceremonial law in the Old Testament Scriptures. Is circumcision and abstaining from pork all that big a deal? The
orthodox Jews to this day, as well as the Seventh Day Ad-
ventist and Muslims, strictly follow the "ceremonial law" with
ease and enjoyment. Such a view really does make sense to
us. The yoke that Paul is talking about is a yoke that is *impossible to bear*, but many have born the so called
"ceremonial law" without ever considering it a bondage. The
"back to nature" people in our generation follow the ceremonial laws of the Old Covenant almost to the letter and
never complain of "bondage." Their constant cry is the joy
and freedom they have found. And these people do not even
profess to be doing this out of love to God. No, this yoke
is somehow connected to the blood atonement of Christ. It
has to do with something far more serious than mere cer-

emonies. John Stott has the best comments that I ever read
on this passage of Scripture:

> As the New English Bible puts it, *"Christ set us free,
> to be free men."* Our former state is portrayed as a
> slavery, Jesus Christ as a liberator, conversion as an
> act of emancipation and the Christian life as a life
> of freedom. This freedom, as the whole Epistle and
> this context make plain, is not primarily a freedom
> *from sin*, but rather *from the law*. What Christ has
> done in liberating us, according to Paul's emphasis
> here, is not so much to set our will free from the
> bondage of sin as to set our *conscience* free from the
> *guilt* of sin. The Christian freedom he describes is
> *freedom of conscience*, freedom from the *tyranny* of
> the LAW, the dreadful struggle to keep the law, with
> a view to winning the favor of God. It is the freedom
> of acceptance with God and of access to God through
> Christ.[14]

In a parallel passage, Acts 15, the Holy Spirit clearly tells
us what this yoke of bondage is. It is nothing less than tell-
ing a sinner that he must earn his own righteousness. It is
imposing the Tablets of Stone on the conscience as the
"accuser and excuser." Making the Ten Commandments to
be the doorkeeper guarding God's throne is a yoke on the
conscience that no one bear. It is resurrecting the ministry
of the Ark of the Covenant in the Tabernacle and putting
it into the Church. The subject discussed at the Jerusalem
Council in Acts 15 was not primarily the "rule of life for a
Christian," but "What must a sinner do to be saved." Acts
15:1,5 settles what the discussion was all about. The
"believing" Pharisees were insisting that the Gentiles must
be circumcised and keep the law, not to be sanctified, but
to be *saved!*

---

[14]The Message of Galatians, by John R Stott, IVP, p. 132.

In verse 8-11, Peter declares that the hearts of the Gentiles had been "purified by faith." They, like the true believing Jews, had been saved by faith alone without the law. His conclusion is simple and clear. *"Why tempt ye God, to put a **yoke** upon the neck of the disciples, which neither **we** nor our fathers are **able to bear.**" Now what yoke is this? Whatever it is, the Gospel delivered us from its bondage. It is the same yoke that Paul warns us against in Gal 5:1. It is the yoke the men in Acts 15:1,5 were trying to impose on the Gentiles. And exactly what were they trying to impose? They were distinctly saying that you had to obey the law to be saved!* They were putting the law between the sinner and the Savior. They were making the Mosaic covenant to be the Gospel. They were adding the law to the Gospel of grace. The "yoke" in Acts 15 cannot be "ceremonial" law but has to do with the conscience striving to find acceptance by works. Later in this same chapter (Acts 15:24-29) the council binds some "ceremonial" laws (mixed together with "moral" law without any distinction) on the Gentiles out of respect to the Jewish conscience.

None of the ceremonial laws were a "yoke of bondage" in and of themselves. Paul instructs believers to sometimes bear the yoke of any or all of the "ceremonial laws" in order to keep a weak brother from stumbling (Rom. 14 and I Cor. 8-10). The yoke Peter is talking about in Acts 15; that Paul is talking about in Gal. 5:1; and that Hebrews is discussing in Heb. 9:15 is a yoke that cannot be born by anyone. It is nothing less than the law as a covenant laid on the conscience. It is striving to keep the law in order to gain assurance of salvation. The yoke is the awful realization that we have neither the righteous life that the covenant justly demands nor do we have an acceptable sacrifice to give to God to atone for our guilt. We put this yoke on the conscience whenever we use the Ten Commandment as if they were still in the Ark of the Covenant and not done away in Christ. In doing this, we allow the "written code," or Ten Commandments, to once more "stand against us"

(Col. 2:14) instead seeing the Tablets of Stone forever fulfilled in Christ. The written code stood against us only because we could not meet its just and holy terms. When our Surety met its terms, the "written code" on the Tablets of the Covenant was canceled out.

We must never allow a Judizer to use the Old Covenant "against us." The preaching of the law to the conscience with the threat of life and death is a yoke that only a self righteous Pharisee can pretend to wear. And who ever met a joyous and victorious Pharisee? Circumcision and the "clean food" list is observed by people today who make no claim of being saved and they do not feel the least burden. However, the preaching of the law to the conscience with the threat of life and death is a yoke that only the deluded self righteous Pharisee can bear. And even he cannot wear it with any sense of delight but only with a sense of pride.

We could not possible close this chapter any better than with the following quotation from John Bunyan:

> Therefore whenever thou who believest in Jesus, dost hear the law in its thundering and lightening fits, as if it would burn up heaven and earth; then say thou, I AM FREED FROM THIS LAW, these thunderings have nothing to do with my soul; nay even this law, while it thus thunders and roareth, it doth allow and approve of my righteousness. I know that Hagar would sometimes be domineering and high, even in Sarah's house and against her; but this she is to be suffered to do, nay though Sarah herself be barren; wherefore serve it [the law] also as Sarah served her, and EXPEL HER FROM THY HOUSE. My meaning is this, when this law with its thundering threatenings doth attempt to lay hold on thy CONSCIENCE, shut it out with a promise of GRACE; cry, the inn is took up already, the Lord Jesus is here entertained, and there is NO ROOM for the LAW. Indeed if it will be content with being my informer,

and so lovingly leave off to JUDGE me; I will be content, it shall be in my sight, I will delight in therein; but otherwise, I being now upright without it, and that too with that righteousness, with which this law speaks well of and approveth; I MAY NOT, WILL NOT, CANNOT, DARE NOT, make it my Saviour and Judge, NOR SUFFER IT TO SET UP ITS GOVERNMENT IN MY CONSCIENCE; for so doing I FALL FROM GRACE, and Christ doth profit me NOTHING."[15]

---

[15]*The Law And The Christian*, Bunyan's Works, Baker Edition, Vol. 2, p. 338

The Tablets Of Stone, Or Ten Commandments, As A Covenant Document, Had A Historical Beginning And A Historical End

The moment we say that the Ten Commandments are finished as a covenant, it is impossible for some people to understand what we are actually saying. In their confusion, they think they hear us saying, "Away with the moral law." It does not matter how often or how loudly we affirm our belief in both moral law *per se* and specifically the enduring moral principles of nine of the ten commandments written on the Tablets of the Covenant. That is not enough for these people. They insist that we acknowledge that the Ten Commandments *as written on the Tablets of Stone at Mt. Sinai* are "*the* eternal unchanging moral laws of God." It is all or nothing. It is impossible to even discuss the clear Biblical reasons we have for rejecting such a theological view.

The New Testament Scriptures are clear that the Ten Commandments are finished as a *covenant contract* between God and Israel. We are NOT saying that the morality *contained* in the individual commandments is finished. But we are talking about the Ten Commandments considered as a legal contract, specifically as a covenant document. The moral duties commanded on the Tablets of Stone did not begin at Sinai but the use of those duties as the basis of a covenant did begin at Sinai. Nine of the ten commandments were known by men

and punished by God long before and after God gave them
to Israel as a covenant at Sinai. Every specific duty commanded in the Ten Commandments *except the fourth, or Sabbath, was punished before Mt. Sinai, and likewise, every
commandment except the fourth, is repeated in the NT Scriptures.*

*We may disagree with each other on many things about
the "the law" but we cannot deny that the Bible clearly
teaches the following things:*

1. *Some specific "law" had a historical beginning.*
2. *This same "law" had a historical end.*
3. *The historical beginning of this "law" is always associated with the giving of the Tablets of the Covenant to Israel at Sinai.*
4. The historical ending of this "law" is always connected
   with the *coming of Christ and the establishment of
   the New Covenant.*

It is possible that we totally misunderstand exactly *what
specific law* the Bible is talking but is it not possible to deny
that the above four facts are clearly taught in the Bible. The
Scriptures make it impossible for that law to be anything other
than the Ten Commandments written on the Tablets of Stone
and given to Israel at Sinai as the covenant foundation of their
relationship to God. It cannot possibly refer to the
"ceremonial" law. Nor can it be talking about the "law of conscience." It has to refer to the law covenant at Sinai.

As already mentioned, the historical beginning of the law
covenant recorded on the Tablets of Stone coincided with
the beginning of the nation of Israel. In chapter four we saw
these facts set forth clearly in the texts of Scripture that talk
about the Ten Commandments.

There is simply no way to understand the following passage of Scripture if we deny that the law has both a historical
beginning and historical ending:

*For **before the law was given**, sin was in the world.*

*But sin is not taken into account **when there is no law.***

Rom. 5:13

*The **law was added** so that the trespass might increase. But where sin increased, grace increased all the more.*

Rom. 5:20

*What, then, was **the purpose of the law?** It was **added** because of transgressions **until** the Seed to whom the promise referred had come. The law was **put into effect** through angels by a mediator.*

Gal. 3:19

*So the **law was put in charge** to lead us to Christ that we might be justified by faith. Now that faith has come, we are **no longer under the supervision of the law.***

Gal. 3:24,25

The words "before the law" in Rom. 5:13 cannot possibly refer to anything other than the covenant given at Mt. Sinai. The "law" did not exist before that time. The words "before the law" mean "*before* the law." Those words clearly mean that the "law" had a historical beginning at Mt. Sinai.

The words "the law was *added*" make no sense if the law was already there. The law was added at Sinai or Paul is talking nonsense. The law that was "added" at Sinai had reference specifically to "transgressions." The ministry of the law that began at Sinai *ended* when Christ came. There has to be both a historical beginning and ending to the law or Paul is talking in circles. There was a given point in time when this law "was put in charge" and there was another point in time when we ceased to be any longer "under the supervision of the law."

We must all agree that Paul did not mean that mankind, at Mt. Sinai first became aware of moral laws and received for the first time a consciousness that he was to obey those moral laws. How could we explain the behavior of Joseph as a believer and Abimelech as an unbeliever? How could we understand Paul's argument in Rom. 2:14? No, Paul is not talking about the effects of conscience in these passages.

We must also agree that Paul is not denying that God, before Sinai, punished behavior that was contrary to the moral duties set forth in the laws given at Sinai as a covenant. The flood did not occur because God did not feel well that day. That event was the direct result of men and women living in a manner which they had every reason to know was displeasing to God. They were living in total disobedience to the very moral laws that were "given" to Israel at Sinai. There was a "law" given at Sinai for the first time and there was also a "law" in existence before Mt Sinai. But whatever "law" began at Sinai also forever ended at the cross. However, there is another kind of "law" that continues in the Christian life. If this sounds a bit confusing and contradictory, we are only stating the specific problems that different theological writers find in Paul's habit of using the "law" in several different senses.

It is obvious to us that Paul, in the verses just quoted, is talking about the Ten Commandments purely in *covenant terms*. This has to be the meaning of the word "law" in Gal. 3 and 4. Gal. 3:13,14 tells us that Christ died under the law and delivered us from its curse. That can only be the Tables of Stone. The "law" that came 430 years after the promise to Abraham is, at least on the surface, totally different from the promise of the gospel given to Abraham. The question in verse 21 is only raised because the difficultly is so obvious. The fact that Paul spends so much time in answering the problem with a carefully worded argument proves the reality of a problem. The argument is so careful that it builds a key point on the use of the singular "seed" instead of seeds (3:16). The question in Gal. 3:19 and the follow up questions in verse 21 are both unnecessary if there is no difference at all in the promise to Abraham and the Law of Moses. Why go to such pains to explain the difference between two things if they are the same?

The law in Gal. 3 had the power to "imprison the whole world" and prove it was "guilty before God" (vs. 21-23). The Jewish ceremonial law could never do that. The words in verse 20 can only refer to the giving of the law at Mt. Sinai. The law in Gal. 4:4 is the law covenant under which Jesus was born and under which He died. Gal. 4:24 & 25 removes all doubt as to what Paul means by "the law" in this whole context:

> *These things may be taken figuratively, for the women represent **two covenants**. One covenant is from Mount Sinai and bears children who are to be slaves: **This is Hagar**. Now Hagar **stands for Mount Sinai in Arabia** and corresponds to the present city of Jerusalem, because she is in slavery with her children.*
> Gal. 4:24,25

The moment we admit that Paul, in these passages, is obviously talking about the Tables of Stone on which was written the Ten Commandments, or terms of the Old Covenant, it resolves the whole problem and Paul's statements about the law immediately fit together in perfect harmony. We see that when Paul speaks in negative terms about the law, its weaknesses, or its final demise, he is referring to the law covenant (Ten Commandments) written on the Tablets of Stone. When he speaks of the law in a good sense and applies it to us today, he is speaking of the moral duties contained in the individual laws which continue after the Ten Commandments, as the covenant document, are finished.

The reader is almost sure to be thinking, "That sounds correct. However, if such an easy answer is clearly set forth in the Bible, *why do so many preachers and theologians miss it?*" Some people cannot hear what Paul is saying simply because *it will not fit into the theological system that they have*

imposed on the Bible. In that system, the Ten Commandments cannot be viewed as a distinct and separate covenant
made only with Israel. The Ten Commandments written on
stone tablets at Mt. Sinai simply must be a gracious covenant
and not a covenant of works.

The Ten Commandments simply cannot begin at Sinai in
any sense whatever in that particular system. It is absolutely
essential as the "good and necessary consequence" of
Covenant Theology that the law did not begin at Sinai or the
whole system is destroyed. We are told that the words "Before
the law" cannot be referring to the Ten Commandments in
any sense whatever! The Bible clearly says otherwise.

We will not take time to cover the other verses quoted.
The reader need only read the verses and try to fit his view
of the Ten Commandments into those clear statements concerning the historical beginning and historical ending of the
"the law" and see if they match.

We saw in chapter seven that the Ten Commandments,
or Tablets of Stone, considered as the covenant that was kept
in the Ark of the Covenant in the Most Holy Place, were finished when the veil of the temple was rent from top to bottom (Mt. 27:51). Those Tablets were instantly as obsolete as
Aaron and the sacrifices.

The following facts summarize Paul's understanding of the
purpose and function the Ten Commandments today:

1. A New Covenant was ratified in the blood of Christ
    at the cross. The Old Covenant written on the Tablets
    of Stone at Sinai have been "fulfilled" and done away.
    The claims of the Old Covenant have been met; it's
    curse has been endured and removed; and it's bless-
    ings have been secured by Christ and bestowed on
    His Church.

2. A new people or nation was "born in a day" at Pen-
    tecost. The true "holy nation" of "kings and priests"
    (the true Israel of God) came into being (Compare Ex.
    19:4,5 and I Pet. 2:9-11).

3. A new approach to God was opened up the moment the veil was rent from top to bottom. It was the Tablets of Stone that blocked the way into the presence of God's presence, but now the terms of the covenant written on stone (Ten Commandments) have been fully met and we enter boldly into the Most Holy Place (Heb. 10:1-23).

4. A new status, Sons of God, with new privileges was given to the "grown up" people of God.

5. A new Pedagogue took over in the conscience of the New Covenant believer. The Tables of Stone were, in themselves, the old Pedagogue in the conscience of an Israelite. That old Pedagogue has been dismissed (Gal. 3:24,25) and been replaced by the indwelling Holy Spirit.

CHAPTER 9

The Biblical Significance Of The Tables Of Stone

We have carefully explained and then used Biblical terms throughout this book. We have at various times deliberately used one of the seven interchangeable terms, or synonyms, when we wanted to refer to the Ten Commandments. The term that the Holy Spirit has used most often in reference to the Ten Commandments is "the Tables of Stone." It is one of the only two terms that is used in both the OT and NT Scriptures. The only other term used in both the Old and New Testament Scriptures is the term "the Tables of the Covenant." The Holy Spirit never once used the words "Ten Commandments" in the NT Scriptures but He did use these two synonyms. Both of the synonyms used in the New Testament Scriptures use the words "Tables of Stone" and take us back to the covenant at Sinai. It seems significant that both the Old and the New Testament Scriptures use the word "covenant" when referring to the Ten Commandments (Deut. 9:9 and Heb. 9:4). It would seem that the Holy Spirit wants us to think "covenant" when He makes reference to the Ten Commandments.

The great significance of the Ten Commandments in the Bible is that they were the actual covenant document upon which everything pertaining to Israel rested. The importance of the Tablets of Stone, as well as their unique character, is identical to the importance of the Constitution of the USA. Nowhere does the Word of God call, or treat, the Tables of Stone as the "unchanging moral law of God." It always relates them to Mt Sinai when God made them the basis of the covenant with Israel. We saw this clearly in chapter 4.

It is true that various writers in both the OT and NT Scriptures will quote individual commandments out of the Decalogue (and also out of the rest of the OT Scriptures) and use it to reinforce a moral duty. Our Lord used Deut. 6:6 and Lev. 19:18 as the foundation to prove the two greatest commandments in all of Scripture. Does that mean that the rest of the laws in those chapters are of the same importance?

We are only insisting that when the Ten Commandments are considered as a single unit, as the "Tablets of Stone," they are always viewed as a "*covenant*." The question is never, "Do the Ten Commandments contain unchanging moral law?" Of course they do. We only object when someone insists that the Ten Commandments, as recorded on the Tablets of Stone at Sinai, are 100% unchanging moral law. We realize that some people's system of theology forces them to this position. However, the position is still wrong. We gladly acknowledge that the Tables of Stone *contain* much moral law but we also believe: (1) they contain some ceremonial law; (2) they contain some moral laws that were changed by Christ such as the laws governing marriage, divorce and polygamy.

The real question should always be, "In the mind of the writers of Scripture, what is the great significance of the Ten Commandments?" If we answer this question with Scripture, our answer will always be, "The Ten Commandments are viewed as the terms of the Old Covenant that God made with Israel at Sinai." The Bible never gives the answer, "God's unchanging moral law." Some theological systems may respond in that way but the Scriptures never do.

If the discussion shifts from the Tablets of the Covenant, or Ten Commandments, as a covenant document to any individual or specific moral duty commanded in the "words of the covenant," the questions should change accordingly. We are now discussing an entirely different subject. The question has now become, "Are the Ten Commandments, or Tablets of Stone, *as given at Mt Sinai*, the highest, and therefore totally sufficient moral law for the Christian's rule of life today?" We should answer, "Absolutely Not!" They are not the highest moral law ever given, and they are certainly not sufficient for the Christian's rule of life today. The Tablets of Stone are only a dim shadow when compared to the words of Christ in the Sermon on the Mount.

Each of the commandments written on the Tablets of the Covenant stands entirely on its own merit when considered individually and independently of their covenant status. While some of the commandments remain in force exactly as they were given at Sinai, some of them are changed and raised to a higher level. While some are dropped, or at least totally spir- itualized, others are redefined and enlarged. We believe that our Lord Jesus Christ has every right to make all of these changes. We respect Moses and acknowledge his greatness but we love Jesus Christ and believe that He is far greater than Moses. The Tablets of Stone were indeed the highest moral code ever given *up to that point in time*. But the Sermon on the Mount is a much higher and more spiritual moral code than the Tables of Stone.

The Ten Commandments *contain* much unchanging moral law that is just as binding on us today as it was on an Israelite. However, that is a totally different position than equating the Tablets of the Covenant with a so-called "eternal moral law." The problem is the adamant insistence of some theologians that the Tablets of Stone are, in their *entirety as given at Sinai*, the "highest moral law ever given" and therefore "totally suf- ficient, when correctly understood, to be the Christian rule of life today." This makes it absolutely impossible for them to accept the clear fact that the Ten Commandments are the distinct covenant that established Israel's nationhood.

The Medieval concept of law which breaks it down into moral, ceremonial and civil laws must be replaced with Biblical terminology. "The covenant in force at the time" is the means of establishing morality and holiness for any individual. God's commandment to Israel to "be ye holy, for I am holy" is the identical commandment that is given to Christians today. When Peter exhorts us to be holy, he quotes from the OT Scriptures (Lev. 11:44-46; 19:2; 20:7, etc.). However, carrying out the commandment "to be holy" as given in I Pet. 1:15,16 is totally different from carrying out the identical commandment as given to Israel under the Old Covenant. A failure to see this difference makes it impossible to understand the correct relationship of the laws of the Old Covenant to a believer's life today.

We cannot possibly understand how David could enter into a polygamous marriage with Bathsheba with God's expressed approval and blessing without understanding the change in the terms of the "Be ye holy, for I am holy" commandment when it is given under the New Covenant. Obviously David could be holy in God's sight under the Old Covenant and practice polygamy but a believer today under the New Covenant cannot do the same thing.[16] Polygamy did not break the Seventh Commandment (You shall not commit adultery) under the Old Covenant but it does violate the new and higher moral law that Christ gave the Church in the New Covenant.

We must face the fact that it is impossible to make a clear distinction between moral and ceremonial laws in Scripture. While we would all put eating unclean animals on the so called "ceremonial law list" (Lev. 11:44-46) and would certainly put respecting our parents (Lev. 19:2,3) on the so called "moral list," the Holy Spirit put them both on the same list under

---

[16]See "But I Say Unto You," by John G. Reisinger, for a discussion of the change from the canon of conduct under which Israel lived to the canon of conduct under which the Church lives. It is vital that this change of canons be understood, especially as the two different canons relate to the polygamy and easy divorce allowed under the Old Covenant. This book is available from Crowne Publications, P.O. Box 688, Southbridge, Mass., 01550

the Old Covenant. This is even clearer in Lev. 19:18,19. In these verses, one of the two greatest moral commandments ("love your neighbor as yourself") is mixed together with "ceremonial laws."

> *Do not seek revenge or bear a grudge against one of your people, but **love your neighbor as yourself.** I am the LORD. Keep my decrees. Do not **mate** different kinds of animals. " 'Do not plant your field with **two kinds of seed.** Do not wear clothing woven of **two kinds of material.***
>
> Lev. 19:18,19

In the above passage of Scripture, the Holy Spirit deliberately put the second *highest moral commandment in all of Scripture* right in the middle of what would have to be designated a "ceremonial list." Was Jesus conscious of the immediate context when He took a phrase out of Lev. 19:18 and turned it into the "second greatest commandment" in all of the Word of God? Jesus obviously did not think of the Ten Commandments as the "highest moral standard ever given." The context of the text quoted by Jesus gives no indication that it is a "great moral law" and the surrounding laws are only "ceremonial." Nor is there the least indication in the text that we are to "get ready for a real biggy." Both the first and second "greatest commandments" are almost like off handed statements when seen in their contexts. It is only when Christ chooses to use Lev. 19:18, as He does in Mt. 22, that the phrase in this text becomes the "second highest commandment" upon which all other laws, including the Ten Commandments, hang. Dt. 6:6 and Lev. 19:18 are *not* the "summary of the Ten Commandments." *It is* the other way around!

Let us look at the context of the "second highest commandment":

> *The LORD said to Moses, Speak to the entire assembly of Israel and say to them: **'Be holy because I, the LORD your God, am holy. Each of you must** re-*

*spect **his mother and father,** and you must **observe my Sabbaths.** I am the LORD your God. . . . Do not seek revenge or bear a grudge against one of your people, **but love your neighbor as yourself.** I am the LORD. Keep my decrees. **Do not mate different kinds of animals.** Do not plant your field with **two kinds of seed.** Do not wear clothing woven of **two kinds of material.** . . . Do not **eat any meat with the blood** still in it. Do not practice **divination or sorcery.** Do not cut the **hair at the sides of your head** or clip off the **edges of your beard.** Do not cut your bodies for the dead or put tattoo marks on yourselves. I am the LORD. Do not **degrade your daughter by making her a prostitute**, or the land will turn to prostitution and be filled with wickedness. Observe my Sabbaths and have reverence for my sanctuary. I am the LORD.*
                                          Lev. 19:1-3, 18,19, 26-30.

It is obvious that neither our Savior nor Moses, the writer of Leviticus, thought of dividing up the various laws in Lev 19 into different kinds of lists. The chapter begins with the identical exhortation of "Be Holy for I am Holy" that Peter gives to Christians (I Pet. 1:15,16). The above verses, quoted from Lev. 19, covers honoring parents, keeping the Sabbath, loving our neighbor as ourself (the "second greatest law"), and then immediately talks about mixing different seed and different cloth and cross breading of animals. It is impossible to miss the fact that some of these laws are "ceremonial" in nature and others are "moral" in nature. It is just as impossible to try to create two "lists of laws," one "moral" and the other "ceremonial," out of these verses.

However, the moment we admit this we face a dilemma. No one would dare deny that Lev. 19:18 is, according to Christ, the second highest "moral law" in the Bible. To deny this is to contradict Christ. Likewise, no one would dare try to make the *very next verse*, 19, into a *"moral law."* Was the Holy Spirit playing games with us when He wrote Lev. 19 or does this show us how utterly futile and wrong it is to think in terms of a "moral" list and a "ceremonial" list of laws?

It is amazing that anyone can read Lev. 19:26, which talks about eating blood and witchcraft, then read the next verse, 27, which discusses how to cut your hair and beard, and believe that the Old Covenant laws are divided up into "ceremonial and moral" lists. *All of the laws given* in Lev. 19 were both equally important and equally binding on an Israelite. As the Israelite tried to obey God and "be holy," he was just as duty bound to attach the same importance to his diet and hair style as he did to the treatment of his parents, his observance of the Sabbath, and loving his neighbor. Getting a tatoo mark and making your daughter a prostitute are both given in the same breath without a ounce of difference in importance.

In no way could "love your neighbor as yourself" be the "second greatest moral duty" for an Israelite living under the law of Lev. 19. This duty was no more important than planting his garden correctly. The same thing is not true today. There is a very great difference in the respective importance of those same things under the New Covenant. In other words, *how* an Israelite obeyed the commandment "Be ye Holy" is in many respects totally different from how a Christian today obeys the identical commandment. The way to tell the difference is not by arbitrarily creating a "moral law" list and a "ceremonial law" list. Now, we are NOT saying that there are no *individual* laws that are "moral" in their very nature. Lev. 19:18 is surely such a law. We also believe there are other laws that are "ceremonial" in nature (Lev. 19:19). We are insisting that neither Moses nor Christ, or anyone else, in all of Scripture created lists and used the different lists as the foundation of moral conduct.

Let us summarize what we are saying:

1. There is a radical difference in the specific laws that an Israelite and a Christian follows in order to obey the commandment, "Be ye holy, for I am Holy." Any

honest comparison of I Pet. and Lev. 19 will show this
to be the case.

2. The commandment to be "Be ye holy, for I am holy"
   is identical in both covenants. However, the specific
   laws to be obeyed in order to be holy are not the same.
   There are many instances where the duty is identical
   in both cases but there are also instances where the
   duties are radically different.

3. Anything that is intrinsically "moral" in its very nature
   is always moral. We dare not arbitrarily decide what
   is moral and what is not. We must obey all of God laws
   that He tells to obey simply because He says so. God
   may (and definitely has) take a law that is purely ceremonial in nature and make obedience to that particular law a matter of life or death. Both the Sabbath
   and circumcision are examples of this when God made
   them covenant signs. Breaking these "ceremonial" laws
   were the most grievous sins that a Jew could commit
   simply because they were sins against the covenant
   signs (Ex. 4:24-26 and Num. 15:32-36). Touching a
   dead body was not intrinsically "immoral" but it was
   still a great sin under the Old Covenant. Eating shrimp
   was an issue of "moral disobedience" for an Israelite.

4. That which makes the difference is NOT discovered
   by arbitrarily creating "lists" of different kinds of laws.
   That is simply not possible. No writer of Scripture in
   either the Old or New Testament ever hinted at such
   a method. Our duty to God is defined by the laws of
   the specific covenant under which we live. The Old
   Covenant was accompanied by a whole series of laws
   given at various times through prophets. All of these
   were equally part of the "The Law of Moses" and therefore equally binding on an Israelite because he was a
   member of the theocracy. The New Covenant is accompanied by new and higher laws given by Christ and
   the Apostles and these laws are all binding on a Chris-

tian because he is a citizen in the Kingdom of Christ.

We have not understood the message of the New Testament Scriptures until we see the historical shift from the authority of Moses to the full and final authority of Christ. Christians are not under the authority of Moses as their lawgiver. They are under the authority of Christ the new Lawgiver. Christians are not under the Old Covenant and do not use it to define their moral absolutes any more than they use it to define their diet. They are under the New Covenant and it defines everything in their life and worship either by clear precept or personal application of a principle. Often times the principle will be a spiritual application of an Old Covenant law. Paul's use of Dt. 25:4 is only one example: "Do not muzzle an ox while it is treading out the grain." Is it only about oxen that God is concerned? (I Cor. 9:9)

Christians are in no sense lawless. They are under higher laws and a greater obligation to be holy because of Calvary. The difference in their holiness is the specific laws that they obey.

This is exactly what Paul is saying in the following text:

> *Consequently, you are no longer foreigners and aliens, but fellow citizens with God's people and members of God's household, built on the **foundation of the apostles and prophets,** with Christ Jesus himself as the chief cornerstone.*

Eph. 2:19,20

The "prophets" in this passage cannot possibly be referring to the *Old Testament* Prophets. It is referring to the New Testament Prophets.[17] The life and worship of the Church is not built on Moses, his laws, or the covenant that established Israel as a nation. The foundation of the Church is Christ Him

---

[17]For solid exegetical evidence of this fact see William Henrickson, Commentary of Ephesians, Baker Book House, p 142

self and her life and worship is governed through the laws that
He gives through the Apostles and Prophets. John Stott has
said it better than we can:

> The couplet "Apostles and Prophets" may bring to-
> gether the Old Testament (prophets) and the New Tes-
> tament (apostles) as the basis of the church's teaching.
> But the inverted order of the words (not "prophets and
> apostles" but "apostles and prophets") suggests that
> probably the New Testament "prophets" are meant.
> If so, their bracketing with the apostles as the **church's
> foundation** is significant. The reference again must
> be to a small group of inspired teachers, associated
> with the apostles, who together bore witness to Christ
> and whose teaching was derived from revelation (3:5)
> and was foundational.

**In practical terms this means that the church is built
on** the New Testament Scriptures. They are the church's **foundation documents.** And just as a foundation cannot be tamp-
ered with once it has been laid and the superstructure is being
built upon it, so the New Testament foundation of the church
is inviolable and cannot be changed by and additions, sub-
tractions or modifications by teachers who claim to be apostles or prophets today. The church stands or falls by its loyal
dependence on the **foundation truths which God** revealed
to his apostles and prophets, and which are now **preserved
in the New Testament Scriptures.**[18]

The life and worship of Israel was built on the Old Covenant
and the specific laws that were necessary to administer that
covenant. These laws were given to Israel by the different prophets. The life and worship of the Church is built on the New
Covenant and the laws necessary to govern a community based
on grace and not law. These laws are essential to administer
the New Covenant. Today we find all of these laws in the New

---

[18]John R Stott, God's New Society, InterVarsity Press, p 107

Testament Scriptures. The New Testament Scriptures inter-
pret as well as add to the Old Testament Scriptures. The full
and final authority over the Church's life and worship is not
Moses and the Laws of Israel's earthly theocracy. Our full and
final authority is the Lord Jesus Christ. He expresses and defines His will and authority through His Word, the inspired
New Testament documents. That is precisely what Paul means
in Eph. 2:19,20.

We are not suggesting that the OT Scriptures do not set
forth some laws that are clearly moral in nature and therefore
always binding on all men in all ages. We also agree that there
are other laws that are just as clearly ceremonial that have been
done away in Christ. That is too obvious for anyone to deny.
However, that is far different than creating *clear cut lists*, or
specific codes of law, and: (1) designating one list as "moral"
and another list as "ceremonial," (2) keeping one "list" and
throwing away the other "list."

The Scriptures know nothing of this approach in establishing moral behavior for either a Jew under the Old Covenant
or a Christian today under the New Covenant. The only clear
cut "list" that was written in a codified form was the "words
of the covenant" or Ten Commandments, and that "written
code," considered as a covenant document, was "nailed to the
cross" in Christ (Col. 2:14).

We continue to emphasize that we are saying the Ten Commandments were done away *only when considered a **covenant** document.* We are *not* saying that the morality demanded
in the individual commandment has been done away. Our Lord
Jesus Christ never did away with one single commandment that
was truly "moral" regardless of where that commandment is
found in the Old Testament Scriptures. Christ did indeed drop

some commandments which were ceremonial in nature.[19] The Sabbath commandments is an example. Christ also changed some other commandments by raising them to a much higher level. The Mosaic law of divorce is an illustration of this fact. Christ also added some totally new laws that are only consistent with grace and totally inconsistent with the Law of Moses. This is why Moses could never have written the Sermon on the Mount.[20]

Perhaps it would be good to illustrate what just been said. The American colonies were under the constitution and laws of England up until 1776. On that date, the colonies became the United States of America. They united under the Constitution of the USA. From that moment they were "under a new rule." The laws and constitution of England no longer had any legal authority over any American. The laws of England were totally null and void in respect to us as a nation. None of England's laws could be appealed to as the final authority on any matter whatsoever. America was under the authority of a new document or covenant. The constitution of the USA was now the full and final authority over ever American. That is the exact parallel between the Tablets of Stone given to Israel and the New Covenant given to the Church. Everything that established and governed Israel as a theocracy is no longer in effect over the Church.

It very obvious that the Constitution of the USA carefully considered and used many of the laws of England when they wrote the new laws. However, that is not the point. The only point is the change from being "under the law of England" versus being "under the law of the USA." That is a total and

---

[19]We are not contradicting what we said earlier. We today may refer to a given commandment as "ceremonial in nature" and therefore no longer binding. However, an Israelite would never have done this. He was just as morally bound to obey a food law as any of the Ten Commandments. We can see the difference between "moral" and "ceremonial," and are able to act accordingly. But that distinction was impossible for an Israelite. It was one ball of wax.
[20]See "But I Say Unto You," by John G. Reisinger. This is available from Crowne Publications, P.O. Box 688, Southbridge, Mass., 01550

radical change regardless of how many laws are new or the same. That is precisely what the Bible means when it compares the legal covenant that Israel was "under" and the gracious covenant the Church is "under."

Summary

The Bible always considers the Tablets of Stone (Ten Commandments) as the specific covenant document that established the nation of Israel as a body politic at Mt. Sinai. It was the terms of this covenant document that necessitated and brought into being both the priesthood and sacrificial system that they administered. Everything in Israel's worship centered around the Tablets of the Covenant kept in the Ark of the Covenant.

The first use of the words "the Ten Commandments" in Exodus 34:27,28 gives us the key to the nature and function of their use in the history of redemption. The Tablets of Stone upon which was written the Ten Commandments were:

1. the terms of a legal covenant that promised life and threatened death;
2. the covenant was made only with Israel and established the terms of their special relationship with God;
3. this covenant is the Old Covenant that was replaced by the New Covenant established by Christ.

The Scripture nowhere states or infers that we are to think of the Tablets of Stone as "God's eternal unchanging moral law." We are always to think "Old Covenant." The individual commandments written on the tablets are a different matter. They stand or fall according to their own nature. Nine of the ten are repeated in the New Testament Scriptures and are therefore just as binding on a Christian as they were on an Israelite.

The Ten Commandments, *as given at Mt. Sinai,* are not the rule of life for a Christian today simply because they are not a *high enough standard.* The Ten Commandments, *as interpreted and applied by Christ,* are a very important part of the

Christian's rule of life. However, our new Lawgiver has given new and higher laws in addition to interpreting the Ten Commandments in terms of the kingdom of grace.

It is impossible to separate the thunder, lightning and fear of Sinai from the Tablets of Stone. Until we see that the Old Covenant was forever canceled in the body of Christ on the cross, we have not understood the true nature and function of the Ten Commandments in the history of redemption. The gospel of God's grace cannot remain pure and victorious in the conscience until the covenant of works is replaced by a covenant of grace. A great Puritan preacher, Richard Sibbes, said it well:

> It will prove a special help to know distinctly the difference between the covenant of works and the covenant of grace, between Moses and Christ; Moses without all mercy breaketh all bruised reeds, and quencheth all smoking flax. For the law requireth, 1, personal; 2, perpetual; 3, perfect obedience; 4, and from a perfect heart; and that under a most terrible curse, and giveth no strength, a severe task-master, like Pharaoh's requiring the whole tale, amd yet giveth no straw. Christ cometh with blessing upon blessing even upon those whom Moses had cursed, and with healing balm for those wounds which Moses had made.
>
> The same duties are required in both covenants; as, 'to love the Lord with all our hearts, with all our souls,' &c., Deut VI. 5. In the covenant of works, this must be taken in the rigour. . . .
>
> This law is sweetened by the gospel, and becometh delightful to the inner man, Rom. VII. 22. Under this gracious covenant sincereity is perfection. This is the death in the pot in the Roman religion, that they confound the two covenants; and it deads the comfort of drooping ones, that they cannot distinguish them. And thus they suffer themselves to be held 'under bondage,' Isa. LXI. 1, 2, when Christ hath set open doors

before them.[21]

The Holy Spirit has said it best of all:

You have not come to a mountain that can be touched and that is burning with fire; to darkness, gloom and storm; to a trumpet blast or to such a voice speaking words that those who heard it begged that no further word be spoken to them, because they could not bear what was commanded: "If even an animal touches the mountain, it must be stoned." The sight was so terrifying that Moses said, "I am trembling with fear." But you have come to Mount Zion, to the heavenly Jerusalem, the city of the living God. You have come to thousands upon thousands of angels in joyful assembly, to the church of the firstborn, whose names are written in heaven. You have come to God, the judge of all men, to the spirits of righteous men made perfect, to Jesus the mediator of a new covenant, and to the sprinkled blood that speaks a better word than the blood of Abel. See to it that you do not refuse him who speaks. If they did not escape when they refused him who warned them on earth, how much less will we, if we turn away from him who warns us from heaven? Hebrews 12:18-25

---

[21]Works of Richard Sibbes, Vol. I, p. 58,9.

Bibliography for "Tablets of Stone"

Bahnsen, Greg L. *Theonomy in Christian Ethics*. Nutley: The Craig Press, 1977

Bernard, Thomas Dehany. *The Progress of Doctrine in the New Testament*. London, Pickering & Inglis Ltd., n.d.

Bolton, Samuel. *The True Bounds of Christian Freedom*. London: The Banner of Truth Trust, 1964.

Brown, Colin, editor. *The New International Dictionary of New Testament Theology*. Grand Rapids, Mich.: Zondervan Publishing House, 1976, 1986.

Bruce, F.F. (Frederick Fyvie). *New Testament Development of Old Testament Themes*. Grand Rapids, Mich.: Wm. B. Eerdmans Publishing Company, 1969.

Bunyan, John. *The Whole Works of John Bunyan*. Grand Rapids, Mich: Baker Book House, 1977.

Chantry, Walter J. *God's Righteous Kingdom*. Edinburgh: The Banner of Truth Trust, 1980.

Clouse, Robert G., editor. *The Meaning of of the Millennium: Four Views*. Downers Grove, Ill.: InterVarsity Press, 1977.

Cunningham, William. *The Reformers and the Theology of the Reformation.* London: The Banner of Truth Trust, 1967.

Dabney, Robert Lewis. *Lectures in Systematic Theology.* Grand Rapids, Mich.: Baker Book House, 1985.

Fairbairn, Patrick. *The Revelation of God in Scripture.* Grand Rapids, Mich: Guardian Press, 1975.

Ferguson, Sinclair B. and Wright, David F., editors, and Packer, J.I. (James Innell), consulting editor. *New Dictionary of Theology.* Downers Grovr, Ill.: Inter-Varsity Press, 1988.

Flavel, John. *The Works of John Flavel.* London: The Banner of Truth Trust, 1968.

Gaebelein, Frank Ely, editor, and D.A. Carson. *The Expositor's Bible Commentary: Matthew.* Grand Rapids, Michigan: The Zondervan Corporation, 1984.

Good, Kenneth H. *Are Baptists Reformed?.* Lorain, Ohio: Regular Baptist Heritage Fellowship, 1986.

Hendricksen, William. *New Testament Commentary: Exposition of the Gospel According to Matthew.* Grand Rapids, Mich.: Baker Book House, 1973.

Henry, Matthew. *Matthew Henry's Commentary of the Whole Bible.* Mclean, Virginia: MacDonald Publishing Company, n.d.

Heppe, Heinrich. *Reformed Dogmatics.* Grand Rapids, Mich.: Baker Book House.

Hodge, Archibald Alexander. *Outlines of Theology.* Philadelphia: Presbyterian Board of Education, 1860.

Kevan, E.F. *Keep His Commandments: The Place of the Law in the Christian Life.* Tyndale Press, 1964.

Kaiser, Walter C., Jr. *Toward an Old Testament Theology.* Grand Rapids, Michigan: Zondervan Publishing House, 1978.

Lloyd-Jones, David Martyn. *Studies in the Sermon the Mount.* Grand Rapids, Mich.: Wm. B. Eerdmans Publishing Company, 1971.

McComiskey, Thomas Edward. *The Covenants of Promise.* Grand Rapids, Mich: Baker Book House, 1985.

Murray, John. *Collected Writings.* Edinburgh: The Banner of Truth Trust, 1982.

_____ *Principles of Conduct.* Grand Rapids, Mich.: Wm. B. Eerdmans Publishing Company, 1957.

Owen, John. *The Works of John Owen.* Edinburgh: The Banner of Truth Trust, 1965.

Payne, J. Barton. *The Theology of the Older Testament.* Grand Rapids, Michigan: Zondervan Publishing Company, 1962

Pink, A.W. *An Exposition of the Sermon on the Mount.* Swengle, Pa.: I.C. Herendeen, 1953

Poole, Matthew. *A Commentary on the Holy Bible.* Mclean, Virginia: MacDonald Publishing Company, n.d.

Reisinger, John G. *Abraham's Four Seeds.* Lewisburg, Penn.: Sound of Grace, 1987.

_____ *"But I Say Unto You."* Southbridge, Mass.: Crowne Publishers, Inc., 1989.

Scofield, Cyrus Ingerson. *Scofield Reference Bible.* New York: Oxford University Press, 1909.

Vos, Geerhardus. *Biblical Theology.* Grand Rapids, Mich.: Wm. B. Eerdmans Publishing Company, 1948.

Watson, Thomas. *The Ten Commandments.* Edinburgh: The Banner of Truth Trust, 1965.

Williamson, G.I. *The Westminster Confession of Faith for Study Classes.* Philadelphia: Presbyterian and Reformed Publishing Company, 1964.

   Wright, Christopher J.H. *An Eye for An Eye: The Place of Old Testament Ethics Today.* Downers, Ill: InterVarsity Press, 1983.

Order These Other Informative And Challenging Books

Battle of the Gods, Morey, 316 pgs., $10.95
A comprehensive and unassailable statement of the changelessness, wisdom and sovereignty of God.

Behind the Watchtower Curtain, Reed, $10.95
Written to answer claims made by the Watchtower Organization, expose the false teaching, cultic practices and to lay bare the secrets of the Watchtower.

"But I Say Unto You, . . . ", Reisinger, 96 pgs., $6.95
A very thorough study of the contrasts found in the Sermon on the Mount between the life of an Israelite under law and the life of a Christian under grace.

Death And the Afterlife, Morey, 315 pgs., $12.95
The most significant work on the subject of death in a century. It defends the Christian position that man has an immortal soul.

Here Is Your God, Morey, $9.95
A definitive study of the nature and attributes of God based on Biblical Truths.

Horoscopes And the Christian, Morey, 64 pgs., $2.95
The number one worldwide best seller on astrology from a Christian perspective.

How to Keep Your Faith While In College, Morey, 160 pgs., $10.95
Survival manual for high school and college age students which gives the information they need to be faithful to the Lord while in college.

How to Keep Your Kids Drug Free, Morey, 120 pgs., $4.95
> A practical "How to" manual for parents, pastors, teachers, youth groups and schools which gives a solid Biblical basis for saying "No to Drug Abuse."

Introduction to Defending the Faith, Morey, $4.95
> A survey of the Christian world view and how it applies to history, art, ethics, psychology and marriage.

Reincarnation and Christianity, Morey, 60 pgs., $2.95
> The classic refutation of the arguments used by reincarnations. The first Christian book written against reincarnation.

Sovereignty of God in Providence, Reisinger, 40 pgs. $3.95
> A Biblical study of six basic principles that undergird all of scripture as it relates to human destiny and God's sovereign providence.

The New Atheism And the Erosion of Freedom, Morey, 176 pgs., $8.95
> A solid refutation of all the arguments used by atheists, sceptics and free thinkers against the existence of God.

When Is It Right to Fight, Morey, 143 pgs., $7.95
> The most thorough refutation ever written of pacifism. It upholds the Christian's right to defend himself, his family, and his country.

Worship Is All of Life, Morey, 113 pgs., $5.95
> The only book of its kind. It explores private worship, family, worship, and public worship.

Order Form

Name: _____

Address: _____

City, State, Zip: _____

Prices Are Effective Until March 30, 1990

Book		Qty.	Price	Total
Battle of the Gods	Morey		$10.95	
Behind the Watchtower Curtain	Reed		10.95	
"But I Say Unto You, . . ."	Reisinger		6.95	
Death and the Afterlife	Morey		12.95	
Here Is Your God	Morey		9.95	
Horoscopes and the Christian	Morey		2.95	
How to Keep Your Faith While in College	Morey		10.95	
How to Keep Your Kids Drug Free	Morey		4.95	
Introduction to Defending the Faith	Morey		4.95	
Reincarnation and Christianity	Morey		2.95	
Sovereignty of God in Providence	Reisinger		3.95	
The New Atheism and the Erosion of Freedom	Morey		8.95	
When Is It Right to Fight?	Morey		7.95	
Worship Is All of Life	Morey		5.95	

Subtotal	
Shipping	
MA residents add 5% Sales Tax	
TOTAL	

Shipping & Handling Charges

Order to $10	add $1.00
Order $10.01 to $25	add $2.00
Order $25.01 to $50	add $3.00
Order over $50	add 7%

Please make check payable to:
Crowne Publications, Inc.
P.O. Box 688
Southbridge, MA 01550

Tablets of Stone

DATE DUE